Academic Encounters

2nd Edition

Jessica Williams
Series Editor: Bernard Seal

CAMBRIDGE
UNIVERSITY PRESS

Shaftesbury Road, Cambridge CB2 8EA, United Kingdom

One Liberty Plaza, 20th Floor, New York, NY 10006, USA

477 Williamstown Road, Port Melbourne, VIC 3207, Australia

314–321, 3rd Floor, Plot 3, Splendor Forum, Jasola District Centre, New Delhi – 110025, India

103 Penang Road, #05–06/07, Visioncrest Commercial, Singapore 238467

Cambridge University Press & Assessment is a department of the University of Cambridge.

We share the University's mission to contribute to society through the pursuit of education, learning and research at the highest international levels of excellence.

www.cambridge.org
Information on this title: www.cambridge.org/9781009345521

First published 2007
Second edition 2013
Update published 2022

20 19 18 17 16 15 14 13 12 11 10 9 8 7 6 5 4 3 2 1

Printed in Mexico by Litográfica Ingramex, S.A. de C.V.

A catalog record for this publication is available from the British Library.

Cataloging in Publication data is available at the Library of Congress.

ISBN 978-1-009-34552-1 Student's Book with Digital Pack
ISBN 978-1-107-62722-2 Teacher's Manual

Additional resources for this publication at www.cambridge.org/academicencounters

Art direction and layout services: Kamae Design, Oxford, UK
Photo research: Suzanne Williams

Table of Contents

Scope and sequence

Unit 1: Laws of the Land • 1

	Content	R Reading Skills	W Writing Skills
Chapter 1 **The Foundations of Government** page 4	**Reading 1** From Colonies to United States **Reading 2** A Balance of Power **Reading 3** The Bill of Rights	Thinking about the topic Reading for main ideas Reading for details Personalizing the topic Examining graphics Predicting Applying what you have read Previewing art Reading critically Reading boxed texts	Showing contrast Writing definitions
Chapter 2 **Constitutional Issues Today** page 27	**Reading 1** Freedom of Expression: How Far Does it Go? **Reading 2** Separating Religion and Government **Reading 3** Guns in America: The Right to Bear Arms	Thinking about the topic Reading for main ideas Applying what you have read Examining graphics Reading for details Predicting Scanning	Writing about numbers Giving reasons Topic sentences

Unit 2: A Diverse Nation • 51

	Content	R Reading Skills	W Writing Skills
Chapter 3 **The Origins of Diversity** page 54	**Reading 1** America's First People **Reading 2** Slavery **Reading 3** A Country of Immigrants	Examining graphics Previewing art Reading for main ideas Reading for details Applying what you have read Thinking about the topic Reading boxed texts Predicting Scanning	The passive voice
Chapter 4 **Diversity in the United States Today** page 77	**Reading 1** America's Increasing Diversity **Reading 2** The Nation's Fastest-growing Minorities **Reading 3** The Undocumented: Unauthorized Immigrants	Increasing reading speed Examining graphics Thinking about the topic Reading for main ideas Reading actively Understanding cartoons	Writing descriptions Writing about growth

V Vocabulary Skills	**A** Academic Success Skills	Learning Outcomes
Guessing meaning from context Cues for finding word meaning Expressing permission	Making a vocabulary notebook Using a vocabulary notebook	Write a paragraph about an important right or freedom with a topic sentence and supporting details
Word families Collocations The Academic Word List	Taking notes with a chart Understanding test questions	

V Vocabulary Skills	**A** Academic Success Skills	Learning Outcomes
Words related to the topic Synonyms Guessing meaning from context	Highlighting Taking notes with a chart	Write two paragraphs about contrasting attitudes toward diversity
Suffixes Words related to the topic Using a dictionary	Answering true/false questions Taking notes in an outline	

Unit 3: The Struggle for Equality • 103

Unit 4: American Values • 153

V Vocabulary Skills	A Academic Success Skills	Learning Outcomes
Suffixes Words related to the topic Guessing meaning from context Understanding key terms	Answering definition questions on a test Answering short-answer test questions	Write two paragraphs presenting a point of view on equal rights and equal protection
Synonyms Prepositions with verbs	Reviewing for a test	

V Vocabulary Skills	A Academic Success Skills	Learning Outcomes
Understanding key terms Word families Collocations	Preparing for a test Answering multiple-choice questions	Write a four-paragraph essay on American values
Prepositions Collocations Word families	Responding to a quote Answering true/false questions Conducting a survey	

Academic Encounters: Preparing Students for Academic Coursework

The Series

Academic Encounters is a sustained content-based series for English language learners preparing to study college-level subject matter in English. The goal of the series is to expose students to the types of texts and tasks that they will encounter in their academic coursework and provide them with the skills to be successful when that encounter occurs.

Academic Content

At each level in the series, there are two thematically paired books. One is an academic reading and writing skills book, in which students encounter readings that are based on authentic academic texts. In this book, students are given the skills to understand texts and respond to them in writing. The reading and writing book is paired with an academic listening and speaking skills book, in which students encounter interview and lecture material specially prepared by experts in their field. In this book, students learn how to take notes from a lecture, participate in discussions, and prepare short oral presentations.

Flexibility

The books at each level may be used as stand-alone reading and writing books or listening and speaking books. They may also be used together to create a complete four-skills course. This is made possible because the content of each book at each level is very closely related. Each unit and chapter, for example, has the same title and deals with similar content, so that teachers can easily focus on different skills, but the similar content, as they toggle from one book to the other. Additionally, if the books are taught together, when students are presented with the culminating unit writing or speaking assignment, they will have a rich and varied supply of reading and lecture material to draw on.

A Sustained Content Approach

A sustained content approach teaches language through the study of subject matter from one or two related academic content areas. This approach simulates the experience of university courses and better prepares students for academic study.

Students benefit from a sustained content approach

Real-world academic language and skills

Students learn how to understand and use academic language because they are studying actual academic content.

An authentic, intensive experience

By immersing students in the language of a single academic discipline, sustained content helps prepare them for the rigor of later coursework.

Natural recycling of language

Because a sustained content course focuses on a particular academic discipline, concepts and language naturally recur. As students progress through the course, their ability to work with authentic language improves dramatically.

Knowledge of common academic content

When students work with content from the most popular university courses, they gain real knowledge of these academic disciplines. This helps them to be more successful when they move on to later coursework.

The Content Areas of *Academic Encounters*

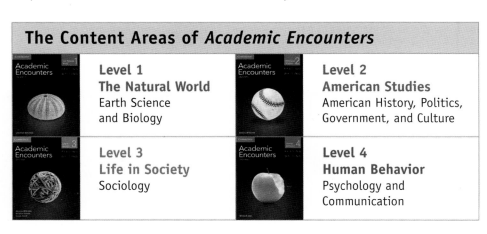

Level 1
The Natural World
Earth Science and Biology

Level 2
American Studies
American History, Politics, Government, and Culture

Level 3
Life in Society
Sociology

Level 4
Human Behavior
Psychology and Communication

Academic Skills

Academic Encounters teaches skills in four main areas. A set of icons highlights which skills are practiced in each exercise.

R Reading Skills

The reading skills tasks are designed to help students develop strategies before reading, while reading, and after reading.

W Writing Skills

Students learn how to notice and analyze written texts, develop critical writing skills, and apply these in longer writing tasks. These skills and tasks were carefully selected to prepare students for university study.

V Vocabulary Development

Vocabulary learning is an essential part of improving one's ability to read an academic text. Tasks throughout the books focus on particular sets of vocabulary that are important for reading in a specific subject area as well as vocabulary from the Academic Word List.

A Academic Success

Besides learning how to read, write, and build their language proficiency, students also have to learn other skills that are particularly important in academic settings. These include skills such as learning how to prepare for a content test, answering certain types of test questions, taking notes, and working in study groups.

Learning to read academic content

PREPARING TO READ

1 Words related to the topic 🅥

Academic texts often contain specialized vocabulary. Sometimes these words may be new to you. In other cases, they may be familiar words with a somewhat different meaning. This text contains some specialized legal vocabulary, that is, words related to the law.

A The text "The Undocumented: Unauthorized Immigrants" describes people who live in a country illegally. Study the definitions and the chart that follows.

Vocabulary related to law

undocumented: without official or legal papers that allow someone to work or live somewhere

unauthorized: without official permission to do something or be in a particular place

deport: to force someone to leave a country, especially someone who has no legal right to be there

Illegal	Legal
undocumented resident	legal resident
unauthorized immigrant	legal immigrant

B Look at Figure 4.4. Use the information to write a sentence about the following:

- undocumented residents
- unauthorized immigrants

2 Thinking about the topic 🅡

Discuss the following questions with a partner.

1. Why do people become unauthorized immigrants?
2. What do you think their lives are like?

Chapter 4 *Diversity in Today's United States*

Reading 1

THE INDIVIDUAL AND SOCIETY: RIGHTS AND RESPONSIBILITIES

Individual rights are so important to Americans and so fundamental to the nation that they are part of the Bill of Rights. The Bill of Rights was written to defend the rights of individuals, to protect them from their
5 own government and against a rule of the majority. Yet a nation that allows all individuals to do whatever they want will soon fall apart. Individuals have rights but they also have responsibilities. It is also important to consider the good of the whole society.

10 A balance between the rights of individuals and the good of society, that is, the good of the whole nation, has been important throughout American history. Sometimes circumstances make it impossible for individuals to accept their responsibilities, and society must act to help those individuals who cannot help themselves. This is one of
15 the most important functions of government. Thus, the United States government has had to find a balance in two situations: (1) between protecting the rights of the individual and protecting the good of society, and (2) between encouraging self-reliance and providing support and assistance to people who need them.

Individual rights versus the good of society

20 Two situations in which the rights of the individual have conflicted with the good of society involve eminent domain and national security. The principle of eminent domain states that private individuals may be required to sell their property, including their homes, if the land is needed for a project that is for the good of society. For instance,
25 the government might want to build a railroad, a school, or a park on land where homes already stand. The owners of those homes receive a payment, but they must cede their property to the government.

The second situation concerns the balance between national security and individuals' freedom of speech and their expectation of privacy.
30 Most citizens do not expect the government to read their e-mail or listen to their telephone conversations. By law, if government officials want to do this, they must first get permission from a judge. Since September 11, 2001, however, the government has limited individual rights in these areas and expanded the power of the government to
35 gather information about private citizens. The government has argued that it must have this power in order to better protect national security.

The Structure of Academic Text

5 The passive voice Ⓦ

The passive is often used to describe a process. In describing a process, key terms can be repeated sentence to sentence to connect the ideas and to create a "chain" of events.

In the example below, the passive is used to describe the steps or process of getting cotton from farms to merchant ships. The chain begins with the key word *cotton* toward the end of the first sentence. *Cotton* then appears at the beginning of the next sentence, which is in the passive. The key words are in **bold** and the passive form of the verb is underlined.

The slaves did the most difficult work; they picked the raw **cotton** from the fields. The raw **cotton** was fed into a machine called a *cotton gin*, which separated the seeds from the cotton fibers, which are called **lint**. Then the **lint** was packed into **bales** that weighed 500 pounds or more. These **bales** were carried in wagons to seaports, where ships waited to take them to factories in Great Britain.

A The description of Triangular Trade below is also an example of a text chain. Circle the three key words that are repeated. Underline the passive forms of the verb.

In the Caribbean ports, the ships picked up molasses, a syrup from Caribbean sugar, and brought it to northern cities such as Boston and New York. The molasses was then made into rum, an alcoholic drink. Some of the rum was shipped to Africa and traded for slaves. The slaves were then shipped to the Caribbean, and the cycle began again.

B Go back to Step A. Draw arrows between the key words that you circled. Note the passive verb that you underlined. Look at the example in the box again if necessary.

C Read each sentence below. Then add a second sentence to create a two-sentence text chain.

1. In factories in England, the cotton was woven into cloth.
_____

2. The sugar was cooked and made into molasses.
_____

3. The ships that returned to the ports in the Caribbean were filled with slaves.
_____

> **Extensive scaffolding** activities teach students the **structure of academic writing.**

> Students learn **key writing skills** such as summarizing and avoiding plagiarism. This early focus **prepares students** for later extended writing tasks.

Developing Writing Skills

In this section, you will learn writing strategies for using information from texts that you have read. You will use charts to help you. You will not write a paragraph, but you will do all of the preparation for it. You will also use what you learn here to complete the writing assignment at the end of this unit.

Expressing ideas in your own words

One of the biggest challenges in academic writing is finding your own words to express ideas that you have read about. Students often want to use the exact words from the text because they think it is the best way to express these ideas. However, it is not acceptable in academic writing to use someone else's ideas as if they were yours. You must present ideas in your own words. Here are some guidelines to help you. It is a good practice to follow these steps every time you read an assignment.

1. Highlight important ideas and details.
2. Take notes on a separate piece of paper.
3. Do not copy sentences from the text. Use your own words to restate what is in the reading.
4. When you begin writing, refer only to your notes, not to the original text.

A In this chapter, you learned about the struggles and journeys of Native Americans, enslaved Africans, and immigrants. Although the experiences of these people were very different, all of them faced many hardships. Think about the differences and similarities of the experiences of these three groups of people.

B Make notes to prepare for the following writing assignment:

Describe the ways in which hardships were similar or different across the three groups.

Begin by reviewing all three texts. Highlight the parts that are relevant to the assignment. Remember: Highlight only the most important facts and ideas.

C Review the chart below. The first column lists categories of challenges and hardships that the three groups faced. Study these categories and review the material that you highlighted in the texts.

	Native Americans	Enslaved Africans	Immigrants
Government laws and policies			
Working conditions			
Physical violence and mistreatment			
Cultural differences			
Attitudes of other groups			
Other			

Immersive Skill Building

Reading 2

SEPARATING RELIGION AND GOVERNMENT

The men who wrote the U.S. Constitution wanted to prevent conflicts among religious groups, which were common in many countries in Europe at that time. They decided that a complete separation of religion and government was the best way to avoid these problems. This principle is referred to as the separation of church and state.

The First Amendment to the Constitution supports the idea that religious beliefs are a personal choice. It states that the government may not interfere with people's private religious beliefs. The government may not establish a church or force people to practice a particular religion. It may not favor or support one religion more than another. In general, this means that religious practices and symbols are not permitted on government property, such as courts or public (government-supported) schools. For example, teachers in public schools may not say prayers in class. This guarantee of religious freedom also means that individuals may not impose their religious beliefs on others. In other words, they cannot force people to believe what they do. Everyone is free to practice his or her own religion or no religion at all. Some Americans do not like this. They believe that the United States began as a Christian nation and should still follow Christian ideas. Although there is more religious diversity in the United States today than when the nation began, the majority of Americans consider themselves Christians (see Figure. 2.1).

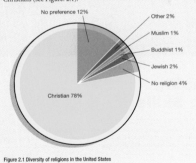

- No preference 12%
- Other 2%
- Muslim 1%
- Buddhist 1%
- Jewish 2%
- No religion 4%
- Christian 78%

Figure 2.1 Diversity of religions in the United States

Chapter 2 Constitutional Issues

> The full-color **design mirrors university textbooks**, ensuring that students not only practice reading authentic texts, but also receive an **authentic university experience.**

AFTER YOU READ

1 Scanning Ⓡ

You will often need to scan when studying for a test or preparing to write an assignment. Scanning a text means reading quickly to find specific information, often facts or statistics. When you scan, you do not read every word. Your eyes pass over the text, stopping only when you find the information you are looking for.

Scan the reading to find the answers to the following questions.

1. What were two dangers that early settlers faced in America?
2. What is the definition of *militia*?
3. Do most Americans believe the narrow or broad interpretation of the Second Amendment?
4. How many guns are in U.S. homes?
5. How many people were killed in the 2012 shooting?

2 Topic sentences Ⓦ

Remember that the topic sentence of a paragraph tells the reader what will be discussed in the rest of the paragraph. It gives the topic and the main point of the paragraph. A good topic sentence should be a general statement, not a statement that is too specific or too emotional.

A Which statement would be the best topic sentence for a paragraph about reasons *against* gun control? Write an *A* (against) next to the statement.

_____ 1. Gun-related deaths are higher in the United States than in any other country.
_____ 2. Americans have strong opinions about gun ownership.
_____ 3. There are several important reasons why many Americans oppose gun control.
_____ 4. Citizens should be allowed to carry guns for protection against criminals.
_____ 5. Many Americans think that ordinary people should not own or carry guns.
_____ 6. There is a clear relationship between gun ownership and gun-related deaths.
_____ 7. Gun ownership is guaranteed by the Second Amendment, and no one can take this right away.
_____ 8. Americans love guns.

B Which statement in Step A would be the best topic sentence for a paragraph about reasons *for* gun control? Write an *F* (for) next to the statement.

C Compare your answers to Steps A and B as a class or in small groups. Explain why the sentences you did not choose are unacceptable topic sentences.

Chapter 2 Constitutional Issues Today **43**

> Throughout each unit, **explanatory boxes describe each skill** and help **students understand why it is important.**

Academic Vocabulary and Writing

Chapter 1 Academic Vocabulary Review

The following words appear in the readings in Chapter 1. They all come from the Academic Word List, a list of words that researchers have discovered occur frequently in many different types of academic texts. For a complete list of all the Academic Word List words in this chapter and in all the readings in this book, see the Appendix on pp. 000–000.

assistance	establishment	guarantees	removed
consists	framework	maintain	revolutionary
documents	fundamental	rejected	specifies

Complete the sentences with words from the list.

1. The Constitution provides a _____ for a government and its major branches.
2. The writers of the Constitution designed the three branches to _____ a balance of power in the government.
3. The Bill of Rights _____ of 10 short amendments.
4. The settlers _____ the king's demand for taxes on stamps and sugar.
5. The police _____ the burning car from the street.
6. When you travel, you should keep your important _____ , such as your passport, in a safe place.
7. Many experts believe that freedom of expression is the most _____ of all rights.
8. If you are in trouble, you should ask the police for _____
9. The First Amendment _____ the right to practice any religion or no religion at all.
10. The Constitution _____ the responsibilities of each branch of government.

Academic vocabulary development is **critical to student success**. Each unit includes **intensive vocabulary practice**, including words from the Academic Word List.

Developing Writing Skills

In this section, you will learn about topic sentences, which are an important part of every paragraph. You will learn to identify, choose, and write topic sentences. You will also use what you learn here to complete the writing assignment at the end of this unit.

Topic Sentences

Paragraphs are usually organized around one idea, and everything in the paragraph should be related to that idea. When you read, you will find this idea in the topic sentence. When you write a paragraph, you should start by writing a topic sentence. A topic sentence does several things.

- It states the topic of the paragraph, or what the paragraph will be about.
- It makes a claim about the topic. That is, it makes an important or interesting point about the topic and is not a simple fact. The reader will expect the paragraph to support this claim.

A Work with a partner. Read the paragraphs below. Find the topic sentence in each paragraph. Underline it.

1. One of the main purposes of the Bill of Rights was to limit the power of government, but this idea is also clear in some more recent amendments. One recent example is the Twenty-Second Amendment. It was ratified, or approved, in 1951. It states that the president can have only two terms in office. In other words, a president can serve for no longer than eight years. Before this amendment, only one president served more than two terms: Franklin Roosevelt, who was elected to four terms. Some people believed that this made the president too powerful, so they proposed the Twenty-Second Amendment.
2. There have been 17 amendments to the Constitution since the Bill of Rights. One of the most important and powerful is the Fourteenth Amendment. One part of this amendment is called the *equal protection clause.* It says that every state must provide equal protection to everyone in the state. This idea was used to argue that separate schools for black and white children means unequal treatment. The Supreme Court accepted this argument. They ruled that separate schools were unconstitutional, based on the Equal Protection Clause of the Fourteenth Amendment.
3. Amending the Constitution is a long and complex process, so it does not happen very often. However, repealing, that is, reversing, an amendment is even more uncommon. It has happened only once. The Eighteenth Amendment, ratified in 1919, prohibited the manufacture and sale of alcohol. Americans did not stop drinking, however. Instead they bought illegal alcohol. In 1933, another amendment, the Twenty-First, was ratified. It repealed the Eighteenth Amendment and ended the prohibition of alcohol.

Students complete each unit by **applying their skills** and knowledge in an extended writing task that **replicates university coursework.**

To the student

Welcome to *Academic Encounters 2 Reading and Writing: American Studies!*

The *Academic Encounters* series gets its name because in this series you will encounter, or meet, the kinds of *academic* texts (lectures and readings), *academic* language (grammar and vocabulary), and *academic* tasks (taking tests, writing papers, and giving presentations) that you will encounter when you study an academic subject area in English. The goal of the series, therefore, is to prepare you for that encounter.

The approach of *Academic Encounters 2 Reading and Writing: American Studies,* may be different from what you are used to in your English studies. In this book, you are asked to study an academic subject area and be responsible for learning that information, in the same way as you might study in a college or university course. You will find that as you study this information, you will at the same time improve your English language proficiency and develop the skills that you will need to be successful when you come to study in your own academic subject area in English.

In *Academic Encounters 2 Reading and Writing: American Studies*, for example, you will learn:

- how to read academic texts
- ways to think critically about what you read
- how to write in an academic style
- methods of preparing for tests
- strategies for dealing with new vocabulary
- note-taking and study techniques

This course is designed to help you study in English in *any* subject matter. However, because during the study of this book, you will learn a lot of new information about research findings and theories in the field of sociology, you may feel that by the end you have enough background information to one day take and be successful in an introductory course in sociology in English.

We certainly hope that you find *Academic Encounters 2 Reading and Writing: American Studies* useful. We also hope that you will find it to be enjoyable. It is important to remember that the most successful learning takes place when you enjoy what you are studying and find it interesting.

Author's acknowledgments

Many people's efforts have gone into this second edition of *Academic Encounters: American Studies.* We have received feedback from many teachers who used the first edition on how to improve it. I hope and believe the second edition is the better for all of their advice. First, I must thank Bernard Seal, series editor, for his ongoing support and counsel. I also want to acknowledge the contributions of all of the fine people on the editorial side, who have improved the text in ways I probably don't even realize: Christopher Sol Cruz, Susan Johnson, Caitlin Mara, Robin Berenbaum. Finally, although she is now happily retired, I must acknowledge the guiding hand of Kathleen O'Reilly on the first edition of the book, without which there would be no second edition.

Jessica Williams

Publisher's acknowledgments

The first edition of *Academic Encounters* has been used by many teachers in many institutions all around the world. Over the years, countless instructors have passed on feedback about the series, all of which has proven invaluable in helping to direct the vision for the second edition. More formally, a number of reviewers also provided us with a detailed analysis of the series, and we are especially grateful for their insights. We would therefore like to extend particular thanks to the following instructors:

Doreen Ewert, Indiana University, Bloomington, Indiana
Veronica McCormack, Roxbury Community College, Roxbury Crossing, Massachusetts
Kathleen Pappert, Laney College, Oakland, California
John Stasinopoulos, College of DuPage, Glen Ellyn, Illinois

Unit 1
Laws of the Land

In this unit, you will look at important features of the United States government and its laws from their beginnings in the eighteenth century to the present day. In Chapter 1, we will see how the United States became a country. We will also discuss the documents that are its political and philosophical foundation. In Chapter 2, we will focus on how those documents remain important and relevant to today's issues.

Contents

In Unit 1, you will read and write about the following topics.

Chapter 1 The Foundations of Government	Chapter 2 Constitutional Issues Today
Reading 1 From Colonies to United States **Reading 2** A Balance of Power **Reading 3** The Bill of Rights	**Reading 1** Freedom of Expression: How Far Does It Go? **Reading 2** Separating Religion and Government **Reading 3** Guns in America: The Right to Bear Arms

Skills

In Unit 1, you will practice the following skills.

R Reading Skills	**W** Writing Skills
Thinking about the topic Reading for main ideas Reading for details Personalizing the topic Examining graphics Predicting Applying what you have read Previewing art Reading critically Reading boxed texts Scanning	Showing contrast Expressing permission Writing definitions Expressing permission Writing about numbers Giving reasons Topic sentences
V Vocabulary Skills	**A** Academic Success Skills
Guessing meaning from context Cues for finding word meaning Word families The Academic Word List Collocations	Making a vocabulary notebook Using a vocabulary notebook Taking notes with a chart Understanding test questions

Learning Outcomes

Write a paragraph about an important right or freedom with a topic sentence and supporting details

Previewing the Unit

Before reading a unit (or chapter) in a textbook, it is a good idea to preview the contents page and think about the topics that will be covered. This will help you understand how the unit is organized and what it is going to be about.

Read the contents page for Unit 1 on page 2 and do the following activities.

Chapter 1: The Foundations of Government

A This chapter addresses the origins of the United States, the structure of its government, and the documents that contain its fundamental ideas. Work in small groups to discuss how much you know about these topics.

Choose one or two countries and answer the following questions about each one.

1. Who makes the laws?

2. Are there any important historical documents? What are they?

B In this chapter, you will also read how leaders are elected in the United States. Discuss the following with a classmate and then compare answers with the class.

Think about each country you discussed in Step A and answer these questions.

1. How does a person become the key leader?

2. How do others become leaders?

Chapter 2: Constitutional Issues Today

A This chapter explores the basic rights and freedoms that are guaranteed by the United States Constitution, especially the part of the Constitution known as the Bill of Rights.

Read these statements about rights and freedoms in the United States. Write *T* (true) or *F* (false).

____T____ **a.** Americans are free to say and write whatever they want.

_____ **b.** Most Americans own a gun.

____T____ **c.** Americans can criticize their government.

_____ **d.** The national religion of the United States is Christianity.

B With a partner, list three rights and freedoms that you think all individuals should expect. Then explain your choices to the rest of the class.

Chapter 1
The Foundations of Government

1 Thinking about the topic ®

Thinking about the topic before you read can make the ideas in a text easier to understand.

Look at this picture. It shows some of the first settlers arriving in America in the winter of 1620. Discuss these questions.

1. What is the artist trying to show about the first settlers?

2. What elements of the painting are important? For example, why is the man on the right kneeling?

3. How do you think the settlers are feeling? What are they thinking?

2 Making a vocabulary notebook Ⓐ Ⓥ

A vocabulary notebook is a useful tool for learning new words and phrases. It is important to record the definitions of new words to help you remember them. However, it is also important to record the context of new vocabulary, that is, the words or sentences surrounding the new word(s). A good way to do this is to record this information in two columns. Here is an example:

Word in context
*The **settlers** hoped to have a brighter future.*

Definition
people who arrive in a new place and live on the land

1. Make a notebook or an electronic file for the new vocabulary you will learn in this book.

2. Make a new entry for the word *kneel* in this sentence: *The man on the right is kneeling.*

We the People of the United States, in order to form a more perfect union, establish justice, insure domestic tranquility, provide for the common defense, promote the general welfare, and secure the blessings of liberty to ourselves and our posterity, do ordain and establish this Constitution for the United States of America.

The preamble (introduction) to the U.S. Constitution

Reading 1

FROM COLONIES TO UNITED STATES

The first settlers

Many people from Great Britain and other countries in Europe began to settle in Britain's North American **colonies** in the seventeenth century. They came for different reasons. Some came for religious freedom; most came because they wanted a better life. At that time,
5 European society was divided into different classes. If you were born into the lower class, it was difficult to move up in the world. In the American colonies, the settlers hoped to have a brighter future: to own a farm, to start a small business, to live among equals.

The road to independence

The settlers wanted to make their own economic and political
10 decisions based on their own needs. The British king had a different view, however. He wanted the settlers to accept and obey British laws even though the settlers had no representatives in the British government. The king and the settlers disagreed about many things, especially about money. The king demanded that the settlers pay high
15 taxes on stamps, sugar, and tea. When they protested against these taxes, the king sent his army to force them to obey. So, in 1775, the War for Independence (sometimes called the American Revolutionary War) began. On July 4, 1776, a group of leaders from the colonies wrote and signed the **Declaration of Independence**, which stated
20 the reasons that the "thirteen United States of America" wanted to break away from Great Britain. Finally, in 1783, the war ended and the Americans won their independence.

colony an area of land controlled by a more powerful country, usually a country that is a long distance from the colony

Declaration of Independence a document written in 1776 that states that the United States is a separate country, independent of Great Britain

The United States Constitution

Winning the war was only the first step in
becoming the United States. The Americans had
25 to make some important decisions about their
government: Should each of the old colonies be
a separate country? Should all the states join to
become one big country? Who should govern?
Who should make the laws? They did not want a
30 strong central government after their experiences
of life under a king. Therefore, for several years,
they tried a system with strong state governments
and a weak central government, but it was a failure.

Then, in 1787, a group of leaders met to discuss
35 a new system of government. They wanted a
republic, that is, a government with an elected
leader instead of a king. They wanted a democratic
government, in other words, a system based on the
idea that all men are equal and that the government
40 should represent all of the nation's citizens. The
result was a constitution. The Constitution, which
was adopted in 1789, creates the basic framework
for the whole United States government. One of the most important
points is the establishment of a federalist system, that is, a system that
45 divides power and responsibility between the states and the federal, or
central, government.

George Washington and the Rules of War

George Washington was an officer in the American army
during the War of Independence. He used some unusual
military strategies. At that time, there were general
practices, or rules, for war in Western countries: no
fighting during the winter and no fighting at night or on
holidays. Washington decided to break the rules in order
to win the war. So, in 1776, when many of the British
generals had gone home for the winter, Washington's
men crossed the Delaware River on Christmas in the
middle of the night and surprised the enemy troops.
The result was the first major American victory: the
Battle of Trenton. Washington led the American
military for the rest of the war and went on to
become the first president of the United States.

George Washington

1 Reading for main ideas ®

Understanding the main ideas of paragraphs is an important skill. Most paragraphs have a *topic sentence*. This sentence states the main point of the paragraph and tells the reader what will be discussed in the rest of the paragraph.

A Look at this list of topics in the reading. Find the location of each topic. Write the correct paragraph number in the blank.

1. Factors in the colonists' decision to declare independence — Par. _20_
2. Attempts to start a new government after the War of Independence — Par. _30_
3. Different systems of government — Par. _35_
4. The Declaration of Independence — Par. _15_
5. Federalism — Par. _45_
6. The class system in Europe — Par. _5_
7. The reasons the first settlers came to colonies — Par. _1_
8. The writing of the Constitution — Par. _40_

B Review your answers in Step A, and review the reading. Then choose the topic sentence for each paragraph.

Paragraph 1

✓ **a.** Many people from Great Britain and other countries in Europe began to settle in Britain's North American colonies in the seventeenth century.

_____ **b.** Settlers who came to the American colonies hoped to have a brighter future: to own a farm, to start a small business, to live among equals.

Paragraph 2

_____ **a.** On July 4, 1776, a group of leaders from the colonies wrote and signed the Declaration of Independence, which stated the reasons that the "thirteen United States of America" wanted to break away from Great Britain.

✓ **b.** The settlers wanted to make their own economic and political decisions based on their own needs.

Paragraph 3

✓ **a.** American colonists had to make important decisions about their government.

_____ **b.** Therefore, for several years, they tried a system with strong state governments and a weak central government, but it was a failure.

Paragraph 4

_____ **a.** The Constitution creates the basic framework for the whole United States government.

✓ **b.** The result was a constitution.

2 Reading for details Ⓡ

> Identifying details that support the main idea in paragraphs is an important skill.

Read these details, which support main ideas in the text. Find the location of each detail. Write the correct paragraph number in the blank.

1. A group of leaders met to create a new kind of government. Par. _35_
2. People came to North America for many different reasons. Par. _5_
3. The settlers fought for independence because they wanted a voice in their own government. Par. _15_
4. The leaders had to decide if they wanted a strong or weak central government. Par. _30_
5. Most of the settlers were hoping for a better life. Par. _1_
6. The Constitution establishes a federalist government. Par. _40_
7. The colonies wanted independence from Great Britain. Par. _20_
8. The Constitution establishes a democratic form of government. Par. _35_

3 Guessing meaning from context Ⓥ

> It is important to develop strategies for unfamiliar academic terms in the texts that you read. One important strategy is to look for signals to a term's meaning in the context, or the words and sentences that come before and after the unknown term. Two phrases that signal definitions are *in other words* and *that is*.

A These terms describe different types of government. Find them in the reading.

- republic
- ⊙ federalist system
- democratic government

B In the text, underline the signals to the meaning of the terms in Step A with a partner. Look at the surrounding words and sentences. Does the context help you guess the meaning of the terms? If so, in what way?

C Complete the following sentences based on the information in the text.

1. A republic is _An elected leader instead a King._
2. A democratic government is _All men are equal and the government should represent all of nation's citizens._
3. A federalist system is _Divides power and responsibility between the states and federal or central government._

4 Using a vocabulary notebook Ⓐ Ⓥ

> Guessing the meaning of new words and phrases is just the first step in building your vocabulary. The most important factor in learning new vocabulary is the number of times you think about, read, hear, or use the word or phrase. Your vocabulary notebook can help you study new words.

A Enter any new or unfamiliar words or phrases from Reading 1 in your vocabulary notebook, including the context.

B Say the words to yourself as you enter them.

C Think of a new sentence for the new word.

D As you read new texts, pay attention to see if these new words appear again. If you notice something new or important in the context, make a note in your vocabulary notebook.

5 Personalizing the topic ®

Thinking about your personal connection to a topic can deepen your understanding of the topic. You should do this while you are reading as well as before you read.

A Look at these pictures and read the captions underneath them.

The first U.S. flag. It is the original "Star-Spangled Banner," with 13 stars and 13 stripes for the 13 original colonies.

The Liberty Bell. Many people believe it rang all day after the Declaration of Independence was signed on July 4, 1776.

B The Liberty Bell and the first U.S. flag are important symbols for most Americans. A *symbol* is something that means more than what it is and is different in kind or type from what it represents. The Liberty Bell and the first flag are symbols of the American fight for independence. Discuss the following questions about symbols with your class.

1. What are some symbols in other countries that you are familiar with? Why are these symbols important?
2. Are there any similarities between these symbols and the American symbols in the pictures above? Explain your answer.

1 Examining graphics ®

Before reading a text, it is helpful to look at any graphs, charts (sometimes called *tables*), or diagrams connected to the text. This will give you an idea of the content.

In the United States, power and responsibilities are divided among three branches of government: the executive branch, headed by the president; the legislative branch, or the Congress (senators and representatives); and the judicial branch, which includes the Supreme Court, the highest court in the nation.

A Work with a partner. Look at Figure 1.1 on page 12. The flowchart shows the responsibilities of each branch of government. Match each responsibility listed below to the correct branch of government. Write *P*, *C*, or *SC* in the blank.

P = a responsibility of the president
C = a responsibility of Congress
SC = a responsibility of the Supreme Court

_C_ **1.** has power to declare war
_C_ **2.** makes laws
_P_ **3.** leads the military
_SC_ **4.** decides if laws follow the Constitution
_C_ **5.** makes decisions about government spending
_P_ **6.** appoints judges
_C_ **7.** makes decisions about taxes
_P_ **8.** makes agreements with other countries

B Compare your answers with a partner or in a small group.

2 Predicting ®

It is a good idea to try to predict what the text will be about before you read it. One way to do this is to read the title, headings for each section, and the graphics.

A You have already looked at the graphics. Now read the title and headings in the text. What are they?

B With a partner, discuss what you think the text will be about.

Reading 2

A BALANCE OF POWER

The first settlers

The men who met to write the United States Constitution had a difficult task. They wanted a strong leader; however, they also wanted a representative government. They wanted judges who would be independent of politicians. They did not want any part of the
5 government to have too much power. Therefore, they divided power among three branches of government: legislative, executive, and judicial.

The three branches of government

Although people often think of the president as the center of government, the Constitution lists the legislative branch first.
10 The legislative branch is called *Congress*. It has two parts: the Senate and the House of Representatives. The Senate has 100 members, two from each of the country's 50 states. The House of Representatives has
15 more – 435. The number of members from each state in the House of Representatives depends on the states' populations. The Constitution names just two people in the executive branch – the president and the vice president. In the
20 judicial branch, the Constitution establishes the Supreme Court, which is the highest court, and gives Congress the power to create other courts.

Congress

Balancing power among the branches

The Constitution gives each branch ways to limit the power of the other two branches.
25 For example, the president can veto, or block, laws passed by the legislative branch (Congress). However, if two-thirds of the members in both the Senate and the House of Representatives disagree, they can override,
30 that is, reject, the president's veto. Congress can even vote to remove the president from office if the president does something illegal. Neither of these things happens very often. Finally, the Supreme Court can reject both the laws passed by Congress and the actions of
35 the president if the judges think that the laws and actions are unconstitutional, that is, not permitted by the Constitution. Figure 1.1 shows the relationship among the branches of government.

The White House: the president's official residence

The Supreme Court

The election of the president

Electing a national leader is an important process. Only a small part of this process is described in the U.S. Constitution; other details have
40 developed over the past 225 years. The Constitution specifies that the president must be at least 35 years old and must be born in the United States. It also states that the president serves a four-year term and then can run for reelection. Starting in1951, there has been a limit of two terms. Although the Constitution does not establish **political parties**,
45 there have been two strong parties in the United States throughout most of its history. This two-party system also helps maintain another kind of balance of power.

political party
a group of people with similar political views that competes in elections

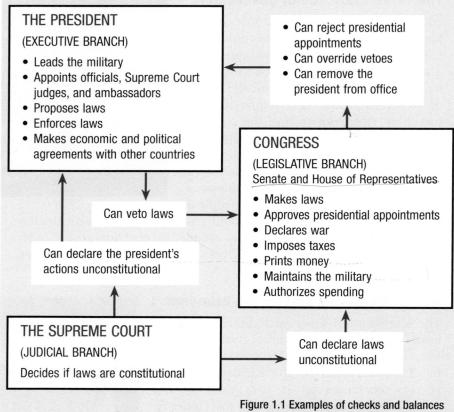

Figure 1.1 Examples of checks and balances among the three branches of government

A federalist system

The U.S. Constitution establishes a government based on federalism, that is, a balance of power between the federal, or central, government and the
50 state governments (see Figure 1.2 on page 14). The federal government is responsible for issues that affect U.S. citizens as a nation. The state governments are responsible for issues that relate to the states. In addition, some powers, such as building roads and paying for public education, are shared by both state and federal governments. Each state also has a leader,
55 called the *governor* who, like the president of the country, is elected by the people. In addition, both governments share certain powers.

1 Cues for finding word meaning Ⓥ Ⓦ Ⓡ

As you read more difficult texts, it is important to try to understand them without stopping to look up every new word. Difficult or key terms are often defined in the text and have cues that signal or indicate a definition is coming. Common cues for signaling definitions include *that is*, *or*, the verb *be*, and parentheses ( ).

A The text contains technical terms about political institutions and processes. Writers may use different signals for the definitions of these technical terms. Review the text for one signal – *that is*. Then highlight the definitions for the following terms:

- override
- unconstitutional
- federalism

B Look at these terms and cues. Write the definition in the blank.

Term	Cue	Definition
1. the Supreme Court (Par. 2)	is	*The highest court.*
2. veto (Par. 3)	, or	*block.*
3. legislative branch (Par. 3)	( )	*Congress.*

C Complete each sentence with a term from Step B or C.

1. The name of the legislative branch is *Congress* .
2. If the president vetoes a law, he *blocks* it.
3. If the members of Congress override the president's veto, they *reject* it.

D Complete the definitions of the words in **bold**. Use information from the text.

1. The Constitution establishes the **Supreme Court**, that is, *highest court* .
2. A federalist system divides power between the **federal**, or *central* , government and the state governments.
3. The Supreme Court decides if laws are **unconstitutional**, that is, if they are *not permitted by the constitution* .

E Now choose your own words to define. Write two sentences that include short definitions. Use *that is*, *is*, *or*, or parentheses ( ). Be sure to use correct punctuation.

2 Examining graphics ®

One frequent type of graphic in academic texts is the Venn diagram. The Venn diagram uses overlapping circles to show relationships. It can show information that is true only for "A" (one circle), other information that is true only for "B" (the other circle), and information that is true for "A + B" (both circles).

A Study Figure 1.2. It is a Venn diagram of examples of the division of power between the federal and state governments.

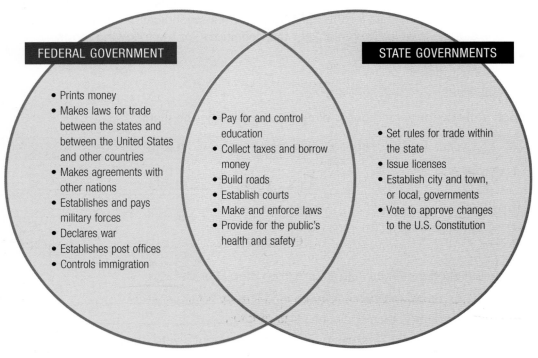

FEDERAL GOVERNMENT

- Prints money
- Makes laws for trade between the states and between the United States and other countries
- Makes agreements with other nations
- Establishes and pays military forces
- Declares war
- Establishes post offices
- Controls immigration

- Pay for and control education
- Collect taxes and borrow money
- Build roads
- Establish courts
- Make and enforce laws
- Provide for the public's health and safety

STATE GOVERNMENTS

- Set rules for trade within the state
- Issue licenses
- Establish city and town, or local, governments
- Vote to approve changes to the U.S. Constitution

Figure 1.2 Examples of the division of power between the federal and state government

B Now read the statements and write *T* (true) or *F* (false).

_F_ **1.** State governments can print their own money.

_T_ **2.** Only the federal government can have an army.

_T_ **3.** Federal and state governments pay for public education.

_T_ **4.** There are courts at both the federal and state level.

_F_ **5.** A state can declare war against another state or country.

_F_ **6.** Only the federal government can ask citizens to pay taxes.

_T_ **7.** There is no federal driver's license; only the states offer driver's licenses.

_F_ **8.** States can issue their own postage stamps and deliver mail.

3 Showing contrast Ⓦ

To contrast ideas is to show the difference between them. The words *however* and *although* are used to indicate contrasting ideas.

However can begin or end a sentence or clause. When it begins a sentence/clause, a comma goes after *however*. When it ends a sentence/clause, a comma goes before *however*.

comma

Congress makes laws. **However,** the president can veto them.

comma

*Congress makes laws; **however,** the president can veto them.*

comma

Congress makes laws. The president can veto them, **however.**

Although introduces a clause. When an *although* clause begins a sentence, a comma is placed at the end of the clause.

clause introduced by *although*   comma   clause

Although *Congress has the power to make laws,* *the president can veto them.*

A Find and underline each occurrence of *however* and *although* in the text.

B Explain two contrasting features of the balance of power in the U.S. political system. Use information from the text and Figure 1.1 on page 12. Write sentences with *however* and *although*. Be sure to use correct punctuation.

C Work with a partner and check each other's work. Make sure the information is true and that the sentences are correctly punctuated.

4 Applying what you have read Ⓡ

Finding ways to apply new knowledge helps you see how well you understand new subject matter.

With a partner or small group, compare the U.S. system of government to the government of another country that you are familiar with. Use the questions below to help your discussion.

1. Is the government based on a federalist system?
2. Are there separate branches of government?
3. How is power balanced among the branches?
4. How are the people represented in government?
5. How many political parties are there?
6. How is the national leader elected?
7. Is the system similar to or very different from the U.S. system?

1 Thinking about the topic ®

A With a partner, read the situations listed below. In the United States, some are legal, or allowed by law, and some are illegal, that is, against the law. Check (✓) the situations that are legal.

_____ **1.** Ms. Taylor is having a party. The police drive by and see the party. They think that some of Ms. Taylor's guests may be selling drugs. They enter the house and search it.

___✓___ **2.** Mr. Jones gives a speech and says that a specific group of people (for example, a racial or religious group) is the cause of many problems and they should be forced to leave the United States.

_____ **3.** Mr. Jones gives another speech and says that the same racial or religious group is the cause of many problems and they should be killed.

_____ **4.** Ms. Johnson, a public school teacher, reads a religious prayer to her class at the beginning of the school day.

_____ **5.** Mr. Stevens tells lies about his neighbor, Mr. Elliot, on an Internet site. He writes that Mr. Elliot is a terrorist. As a result, Mr. Elliot loses his job. Mr. Stevens claims he is free to express his opinions.

___✓___ **6.** Mr. Stone keeps a gun next to his bed at home.

_____ **7.** Ms. Wilson is arrested at her home in California. She is kept in prison for six months. The police do not tell her what crime she is accused of.

___✓___ **8.** Ms. Evans shouts at the president as he passes through a crowd. She says he is destroying the country.

B Explain your answers to the class. Use phrases such as these:

We think it's against the law to _____ because …
I think it's illegal to _____ because …
I believe it is legal to _____ since …

2 Previewing art ®

> Look at the photographs or other art in a text and read the explanations below them. Previewing the art can give you a good idea of what the text will be about.

A Study the photograph and drawing at the end of the reading.

- When the nation was established, not everyone was allowed to vote. Which groups do you think had the right to vote? Which groups did not have the right to vote?
- What do you think were some reasons for these differences?

Reading 3

THE BILL OF RIGHTS

In 1787, the U.S. Constitution established most of the systems and rules to form a new government. However, many leaders thought that something was missing. They wanted to include a completely new idea: the guarantee of individual rights and freedoms and the protection of citizens *against* the government's power. As a result, in 1791, the Bill of Rights, in the form of 10 amendments, or changes, to the Constitution, was passed.

The Bill of Rights is one of the most important documents in U.S. history; its ideas are an essential part of American culture. Although it is only 462 words long (a little shorter than this text), it establishes many fundamental rights and freedoms. When people say, "America is a free country," they are thinking of the Bill of Rights.

The Bill of Rights consists of 10 amendments, most of which can be divided into three basic categories. Some amendments guarantee the rights and freedoms of individuals. Other amendments protect citizens against the misuse of power by the government. Another category of amendments protects the rights of criminal suspects, that is, people who have been accused of crimes.

Guarantee of the rights of individuals

The First Amendment guarantees freedom of religion, freedom of speech, and freedom of the press. This means that everyone in the United States is free to practice any religion or no religion at all. The government may not establish or support any religion. The amendment also guarantees all citizens the freedom to say or write what they believe, even if it is unpopular. There are limits, however. The First Amendment does not protect libel, that is, lies about someone that would harm that person, nor speech or writing that could be dangerous to others. For example, it does not protect speech that encourages people to burn down a building or kill people. However, and perhaps most important, the First Amendment does allow people to protest against the government if they think it is doing something wrong. It permits them to criticize the government in speech or in writing.

Protection against the misuse of government power

The Second and Fourth Amendments help protect all citizens against the misuse of power by the government and, especially, the police. The Second Amendment permits states to form a militia, or army of citizens, and citizens to keep guns for their own protection. The Fourth Amendment forbids police searches without permission from a judge. To get a judge's permission to search a person's home or possessions, the police must give very good reasons.

Protection of the rights of criminal suspects

The Fifth, Sixth, and Seventh Amendments provide protection for
40 people who are accused of crimes. The police may not arrest people
for a crime without sufficient cause and cannot put them in prison.
Criminal suspects have a right to a **speedy** and **public trial** and to the
assistance of a lawyer. They also have a right to a trial that is decided
by a **jury** of 12 peers, that is, ordinary people just like them, instead
45 of a judge.

Amendments to the Constitution: Expanding suffrage

Since the Bill of Rights, there have been 17 more amendments to the Constitution. Three of them expanded suffrage, or the right to vote. The information below shows how voting rights have expanded since the founding of the nation, when only white men who owned land had the right to vote in most states. Look at the questions. Depending on their answers to the questions, people could or could not vote in the United States at one time in the past.

Are you a land owner?

No? ➜ **No voting rights in most states**

Until 1821, many states restricted voting to landowners.

Are you an African American?

Yes? ➜ **No voting rights in most states**

Before the Fifteenth Amendment (1870), states could ban African Americans from voting.

African Americans voting in 1870, shortly after they received the right to vote

Are you a woman?

Yes? ➜ **No voting rights in most states**

Before the Nineteenth Amendment (1920), women were prohibited from voting in most states.

Suffragettes fought for the right to vote for women.

Are you a Native American?

Yes? ➜ **No voting rights in most states**

In some states, Native Americans were not granted citizenship and the right to vote until 1924.

Are you able to read and write?

No? ➜ **No voting rights in some states**

Until 1965, many states required voters to show that they could read and write. This prevented many people with little education from voting, particularly African Americans.

Are you 21 or older?

No? ➜ **No voting rights**

Until the Twenty-sixth Amendment (1971), only people 21 or older could vote.

1 Applying what you have read Ⓡ

Work with a partner or small group to complete the activities.

A Review the text and the three main types of amendments in the Bill of Rights that are listed below.

   a. Guarantee of individual rights

   b. Protection against misuse of government power

   c. Protection of the rights of criminal suspects

B Match each statement below to a type of amendment in Step A. Write *a*, *b*, or *c* in the blanks.

   _A_ **1.** Anyone can criticize the government.

   _B_ **2.** Citizens may own guns.

   _C_ **3.** A person who is accused of a crime can get assistance from a lawyer.

   _A_ **4.** Free speech does not include speech that encourages violence.

   _A_ **5.** Lies that are published and are harmful to others are not protected as free speech.

   _A_ **6.** People are free to practice their religion.

   _B_ **7.** Police may not search a person's home or possessions without a legal reason.

   _A_ **8.** The government is not permitted to support any specific religion.

   _C_ **9.** The police must tell a criminal suspect why he or she has been arrested.

C Go back to Task 1 of Preparing to Read on page 16. Match each situation there to a type of amendment in Step A above. Which type of amendment would help determine if the action is constitutional? Write *a*, *b*, or *c* in the blanks below.

   _B_ **1.**   _A_ **5.**

   _A_ **2.**   _B_ **6.**

   _A_ **3.**   _C_ **7.**

   _A_ **4.**   _A_ **8.**

D Compare your answers to Steps B and C in a small group. Discuss your original responses to the eight situations in Preparing to Read.

2 Reading critically Ⓡ

> You will not always agree with what you read. It is helpful to think about the ideas in a text and compare them to your own knowledge and experiences.

The Bill of Rights provides broad protection to the people of the United States. With a partner or small group, discuss possible negative effects of the Bill of Rights. The questions below will help you get started.

- Are there any cases in which freedom of expression could be a bad idea?
- Is it possible to provide too much freedom?
- Do criminal suspects receive too much protection?

3 Expressing permission Ⓦ Ⓥ

A Verbs of permission express what you may or may not do. Reread "The Bill of Rights" (including the boxed text), and highlight the following verbs of permission: *allow*, *forbid*, *permit*, and *prohibit*.

B Think about the verbs of permission in Step A and what they are expressing. Circle the correct meaning below.

1. **Allow** refers to actions you (*may* / *may not*) do.
2. **Forbid** refers to actions you (*may* / *may not*) do.
3. **Permit** refers to actions you (*may* / *may not*) do.
4. **Prohibit** refers to actions you (*may* / *may not*) do.

C Write a sentence for each right or action listed below. Be sure it is true according to the text. Use a verb from Step B in the affirmative or negative form. Begin each sentence like this: *The Bill of Rights . . .*

1. religious freedom ___The Bill of Rights permits religious freedom.___
2. criticism of the government ___The Bill of Rights allows___
3. freedom of speech ___The Bill of Rights permits___
4. police searches without permission from a judge ___the Bill of Rights forbids___

5. gun ownership ___the Bill of Rights permits___
6. imprisonment without an explanation ___The Bill of Rights forbids___
7. secret trials ___The Bill of Rights prohibit___

D Look at the sentence pattern below. This is the grammatical pattern of the sentences you wrote in Step C.

verb of permission	noun phrase

The Bill of Rights ⌐permits⌐ ⌐religious freedom.⌐

However, the verbs *permit*, *allow*, and *forbid* can also appear in a different pattern.

verb of permission	noun phrase	infinitive

The Bill of Rights ⌐permits⌐ ⌐citizens⌐ ⌐to practice⌐ their own religion.

E Work with a partner and complete the sentences. The first one is done for you as an example.

1. The Bill of Rights **forbids** _the police_ to _search without a warrant_ .
2. The Bill of Rights **forbids** _____ to _____ .
3. The Bill of Rights **permits** _____ to _____ .
4. The Bill of Rights **allows** _____ to _____ .

4 Writing definitions Ⓦ

You will often have to include definitions in your academic writing.
It is important to use a correct format.

A Read the definition below. Look at the format. The XYZ format is common for definitions.

X (term to be defined)	**Y** (general category)	**Z** (description)
The U.S. Constitution	is a document	that established most of the systems and rules for the U.S. government.

B Use the XYZ format to write definitions for the following terms:

1. A criminal suspect is _____ who _____ .
2. Libel is _____ that _____ .
3. The Bill of Rights is a _____ that _____ .
4. Suffragettes were _____ who _____ .

C Details and examples *expand* a definition. That is, they increase the information and make the definition clearer, easier to understand, or more interesting.

> The U.S. Constitution is a document that established most of the systems and rules for the U.S. government. It established the three branches of government: the legislative, the executive, and the judicial branches.

Choose two of the definitions you wrote in Step B and add a detail to them to make them clearer or more interesting.

5 Reading boxed texts Ⓡ

Boxed texts often add interesting information to the material in the main text. They may help you apply the information in the text to your own situation.

Discuss these questions with a partner or small group.

1. Look again at the questions to Task 2 in Preparing to Read on page 16. Were your answers correct?
   - *When the nation was established, not everyone was allowed to vote. Which groups do you think had the right to vote? Which groups did not have the right to vote?*
   - *What do you think were some reasons for these differences?*
2. Did any of the facts in the boxed text on pages 18 and 19 surprise you? Explain your answer.
3. If you were an American, when would you have gotten the right to vote?

Chapter 1 Academic Vocabulary Review

The following words appear in the readings in Chapter 1. They all come from the Academic Word List, a list of words that researchers have discovered occur frequently in many different types of academic texts. For a complete list of all the Academic Word List words in this chapter and in all the readings in this book, see the Appendix on page 206.

assistance	establishment	guarantees	removed
consists	framework	maintain	revolutionary
documents	fundamental	rejected	specifies

Complete the sentences with words from the list.

1. The Constitution provides a _framework_ for a government and its major branches.
2. The writers of the Constitution designed the three branches to _maintain_ a balance of power in the government.
3. The Bill of Rights _consists_ of 10 short amendments.
4. The settlers _rejected_ the king's demand for taxes on stamps and sugar.
5. The police _removed_ the burning car from the street.
6. When you travel, you should keep your important _documents_ , such as your passport, in a safe place.
7. Many experts believe that freedom of expression is the most _fundamental_ of all rights.
8. If you are in trouble, you should ask the police for _assistance_
9. The First Amendment _guarantees_ the right to practice any religion or no religion at all.
10. The Constitution _specifies_ the responsibilities of each branch of government.

Developing Writing Skills

In this section, you will learn about topic sentences, which are an important part of every paragraph. You will learn to identify, choose, and write topic sentences. You will also use what you learn here to complete the writing assignment at the end of this unit.

Topic Sentences

Paragraphs are usually organized around one idea, and everything in the paragraph should be related to that idea. When you read, you will find this idea in the topic sentence. When you write a paragraph, you should start by writing a topic sentence. A topic sentence does several things.

- It states the topic of the paragraph, or what the paragraph will be about.
- It makes a claim about the topic. That is, it makes an important or interesting point about the topic and is not a simple fact. The reader will expect the paragraph to support this claim.

A Work with a partner. Read the paragraphs below. Find the topic sentence in each paragraph. Underline it.

1. One of the main purposes of the Bill of Rights was to limit the power of government, but this idea is also clear in some more recent amendments. One recent example is the Twenty-Second Amendment. It was ratified, or approved, in 1951. It states that the president can have only two terms in office. In other words, a president can serve for no longer than eight years. Before this amendment, only one president served more than two terms: Franklin Roosevelt, who was elected to four terms. Some people believed that this made the president too powerful, so they proposed the Twenty-Second Amendment.

2. There have been 17 amendments to the Constitution since the Bill of Rights. One of the most important and powerful is the Fourteenth Amendment. One part of this amendment is called the *equal protection clause*, It says that every state must provide equal protection to everyone in the state. This idea was used to argue that separate schools for black and white children means unequal treatment. The Supreme Court accepted this argument. They ruled that separate schools were unconstitutional, based on the Equal Protection Clause of the Fourteenth Amendment.

3. Amending the Constitution is a long and complex process, so it does not happen very often. However, repealing, that is, reversing, an amendment is even more uncommon. It has happened only once. The Eighteenth Amendment, ratified in 1919, prohibited the manufacture and sale of alcohol. Americans did not stop drinking, however. Instead they bought illegal alcohol. In 1933, another amendment, the Twenty-First, was ratified. It repealed the Eighteenth Amendment and ended the prohibition of alcohol.

B Review the topic sentences that you underlined in Step A and think about each paragraph's topic.

Paragraph 1 Topic: Limits on government power in the Constitution
Paragraph 2 Topic: The Fourteenth Amendment
Paragraph 3 Topic: Repealing amendments

Now go back to Step A and with your partner, underline the claim that the topic sentence makes about the topic of each paragraph.

C Check (✓) the statements below that make good topic sentences.

> Remember that a topic sentence must:
> • be more than just a fact
> • make a claim that you can support

_____ **1.** The Twenty-Third Amendment was ratified in 1933.
_____ **2.** The Bill of Rights limits the power of government.
_____ **3.** The Constitution has 27 amendments.
_____ **4.** The Fourteenth Amendment contains the equal protection clause.
_____ **5.** The Fourteenth Amendment has provided arguments for important Supreme Court decisions.
_____ **6.** The Eighteenth Amendment resulted in illegal drinking.

D Write a topic sentence for each topic. Then compare your work with a partner.

a. The Constitution
b. The first settlers in the United States
c. Freedom of expression
d. Criminal suspects
e. Voting rights
f. (Choose your own topic.)

Chapter 2
Constitutional Issues Today

PREPARING TO READ

Thinking about the topic ®

A Look at the photographs and read the captions.

Political protestors sometimes burn the U.S. flag to express their ideas.

Burning a cross has been used as a symbol of hatred against nonwhites and non-Christians.

B Discuss these questions with your classmates.

1. Are the activities in these photographs legal in the United States? Why or why not? yes

2. Are these forms of expression legal or acceptable in other countries that you are familiar with? Explain your answer.

3. You can use expressions such as these in your discussion.

I think it is (il)legal for people to . . . because . . .
In my opinion, . . . is (un)acceptable because . . .

C With your classmates, discuss whether there should be limits on a person's freedom of expression. For example, should you be allowed to insult another person's religion?

We the people of the United States, in order to form a more perfect union, establish justice, insure domestic tranquility, provide for the common defense, promote the general welfare, and secure the blessings of liberty to ourselves and our posterity, do ordain and establish this Constitution for the United States of America.

Reading 1

FREEDOM OF EXPRESSION: HOW FAR DOES IT GO?

Since the First Amendment was written, the term *freedom of speech* has gained a broader interpretation. It includes more than what people say. It also includes other forms of expression, such as what people write or do. Most people support the free expression of ideas that they
5 agree with, but the First Amendment is important because it protects the freedom to express ideas that many people do not like. However, there are limits on this freedom of expression.

There are two types of protected free speech that are especially controversial. One of these is hate speech. Throughout American
10 history, immigrants, and ethnic, racial, and religious minorities have often been treated badly. Other Americans have sometimes said or written negative and hurtful things about them. This kind of expression is called *hate speech*. Hate speech is directed against a group of people because of a specific characteristic, such as their race
15 or ethnicity.

Is hate speech constitutional? Are people in the United States permitted to say offensive and hurtful things about Jews, African Americans, Muslims, or homosexuals? In fact, the First Amendment allows this. There are some restrictions, however. If the speech or
20 writing is threatening, it is not permitted. For example, a person can stand up at a meeting and say, "I hate African Americans. I don't want any African Americans in my neighborhood." This is protected speech. However, if the person telephones or sends an e-mail with the same message to an African-American family who lives on his street,
25 this might be a threat. It would not be protected speech.

The First Amendment also protects actions that are similar to hate speech. Some groups in the United States have used burning crosses as a symbol of hatred of nonwhites and non-Christians. The Supreme Court decided the First Amendment also protects people's rights to use symbols, even burning crosses, to express their ideas. However, the use of symbols, such as burning crosses, to encourage violence is illegal.

Protests against the government are also often controversial. In 2011–2012, many Americans participated in the **Occupy movement**. They were protesting against social and economic inequality and, especially, against the government's role in it. They lived in public parks for days as part of their protest. They could do this because they were expressing their opinions. Like symbols, protest is considered a form of speech. However, as with other forms of speech, there are limits on political protest. Protestors cannot stop other people from doing what they want to do, such as going to work or to school. They cannot block public streets or buildings. They cannot prevent businesses and offices from operating. They may not cause harm to the health and safety of others. The police ended some of the Occupy protests for these reasons.

A more extreme form of political protest is the burning of the American flag. People who want to protest against the government sometimes burn the flag to express their opinion. This action angers and offends many Americans. However, the Supreme Court has ruled that flag burning is a legal form of political protest.

Occupy movement a protest movement against social and economic inequality focusing on banks and financial systems

Protestors in the Occupy movement

Global hate speech

The very strong protection of free speech, even hate speech, in the United States is somewhat unusual. Many other countries have laws that prohibit this kind of speech and behavior. Australia, Canada, France, Germany, Great Britain, India, the Netherlands, Singapore, South Africa, and Sweden all prohibit hate speech.

However, hate speech cannot always be kept within national borders, and the Internet has made the issue more complicated. First, people all over the world can read material on the Internet; it does not matter if the Web site is in the United States, Japan, or any other country. It is not clear which country's laws these Web sites must follow. Second, the Internet allows people to hear speech that, in the past, they would never have heard. One example comes from South Africa. A young black leader there sang a song about freedom for the black population in that country. Unfortunately, the song also contained words about violence toward the white population. Someone filmed the performance and put the video on YouTube. The video frightened white people in South Africa. The young man said he did not intend the public to hear it, but he was charged with hate speech and brought to trial anyway.

1 Reading for main ideas Ⓡ

> Understanding how to identify main ideas is an essential reading skill. You must be able to quickly identify the main topic of a paragraph. You also have to be able to identify the main idea of the whole text – the point that the writer is trying to make.

A Read this list of topics in the reading. Find the location of each topic. Look quickly. Write the number of the paragraph (2–6) in the blank.

1. The limits on hate speech   Par. _20_
2. An extreme form of protest against the government   Par. _50_
3. What hate speech means   Par. _15_
4. The use of symbols as a form of free speech   Par. _30_
5. Political protest as a form of free speech   Par. _35_

B Check (✓) the statement that expresses the main idea of the whole text.

_____ 1. Free speech does not include speech that encourages violence.

_✓_ 2. Freedom of speech is broad enough to protect unpopular and offensive ideas.

_____ 3. Freedom of speech has always been the law in the United States.

_____ 4. Freedom of speech includes protests.

C Compare your answer with a partner. Then underline the sentence in the text that states the main idea you chose in Step B.

2 Taking notes with a chart Ⓐ

> It can be useful to make a chart when you take notes on a reading. You can use these charts to help you study for a test. You do not need to write full sentences in a chart.

A Review the reading for examples of expressions that are protected or prohibited. Then work with a partner to complete the chart. Include two situations in which speech or symbols are prohibited and two in which they are protected.

	Protected	Prohibited
Hate speech and symbols	Use symbols	Call ong send e-mails.
Political protest	Live in public, like in parks.	Stop people going to work or school. Block public streets.

B Write two sentences that explain the kind of speech that is not protected by the First Amendment. You can use language such as:

The First Amendment does not protect hate speech that is/if it . . .
There is no protection for political protests that . . .

3 Word families Ⓥ Ⓦ

Academic texts often contain several forms of the same term in a discussion of a subject. These related forms are frequently nouns and adjectives. There are several common suffixes that can change a noun into an adjective. Recognizing these suffixes can help you understand academic texts and extend your vocabulary when you write. Sometimes there are spelling changes in the noun before these common suffixes:

-(i)al   -ful   -ous

Notes

The suffix *-ial* is a variant of the suffix *-al*.

Always check spelling in a dictionary.

A Read the noun and adjective forms of words from the reading in the box below. Then choose the correct form to complete the sentences that follow.

Noun	Adjective
race	racial
controversy	controversial
globe	global
politics	political
religion	religious
hurt	hurtful

1. Microsoft is a _global_ company with offices in many countries.
2. In the United States, all _religious_ groups are free to practice their own beliefs.
3. Hate speech is often directed against African Americans because of their _race_ .
4. Friends sometimes say _hurtful_ things to each other in arguments, but later they say they are sorry.
5. Flag burning is always a powerful form of protest and usually causes a _controversy_ .
6. Most forms of _political_ protest are protected by the Constitution.

B Write the adjective form for the nouns below. Be sure to make the appropriate spelling changes in the noun before adding the suffix.

1. harm   *harmful*
2. danger   *dangerous*
3. president   *presidential*
4. center   *central*
5. pain   *painful*
6. courage   *courageous*

4 Collocations Ⓥ

When you read in English, you will notice that some words often appear together. For example, some verbs almost always appear with the same prepositions. It is important to learn these word combinations. They will help you read more quickly and write more naturally.

A Find the verbs below in the text. Underline the preposition that is used with each of them.

- agree (Line 5)
- participated (Line 34)
- protesting (Line 35)

B Write a new sentence for each verb + preposition combination.

5 Applying what you have read Ⓡ

Discuss these questions in a small group.

A Do you think citizens should be able to do the following things? Why or why not?

× **a.** Join an Internet discussion group that favors the violent defeat of the government
× **b.** Display a sign that expresses racial hatred
× **c.** Publish pictures of people in private situations
× **d.** Insult government officials in public
✓ **e.** Publish private (but true) information about government officials that would make them feel uncomfortable
× **f.** Publish instructions on the Internet for building a bomb
× **g.** Publish government secrets

B At the beginning of the chapter, you discussed what the limits of freedom of expression should be. Continue your discussion with your group.

a. Have you changed your mind? Explain your answer.

b. How does the Internet complicate the answer? Think about how social media sites such as Facebook and Twitter may affect your answer.

Examining graphics ⓡ

Look at the graphs about religion in the United States and other countries. Then discuss the questions with a partner or small group.

1. What do the graphs tell you about the importance of religion in the United States?
2. Would you describe the United States as a religious country? Why or why not?
3. How does the information in these graphs compare with other countries that you are familiar with?
4. Does any of the information surprise you?

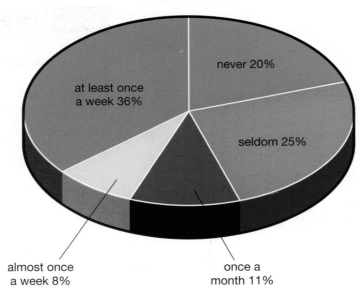

Religious attendance reported by Americans in 2010

never 20%

at least once a week 36%

seldom 25%

almost once a week 8%

once a month 11%

Source: Gallup

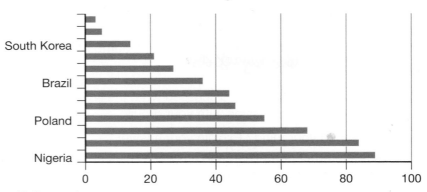

Percentage of regular attendance at a religious service

South Korea

Brazil

Poland

Nigeria

0   20   40   60   80   100

Source: Nationmaster

Reading 2

SEPARATING RELIGION AND GOVERNMENT

The men who wrote the U.S. Constitution wanted to prevent conflicts among religious groups, which were common in many countries in Europe at that time. They decided that a complete separation of religion and government was the best way to avoid these problems. This
5 principle is referred to as the separation of church and state.

The First Amendment to the Constitution supports the idea that religious beliefs are a personal choice. It states that the government may not interfere with people's private religious beliefs. The government may not establish a church or force people to practice a particular
10 religion. It may not favor or support one religion more than another. In general, this means that religious practices and symbols are not permitted on government property, such as courts or public (government-supported) schools. For example, teachers in public schools may not say prayers in class. This guarantee of religious freedom also means that
15 individuals may not impose their religious beliefs on others. In other words, they cannot force people to believe what they do. Everyone is free to practice his or her own religion or no religion at all. Some Americans do not like this. They believe that the United States began as a Christian nation and should still follow Christian ideas. Although
20 there is more religious diversity in the United States today than when the nation began, the majority of Americans consider themselves Christians (see Figure 2.1).

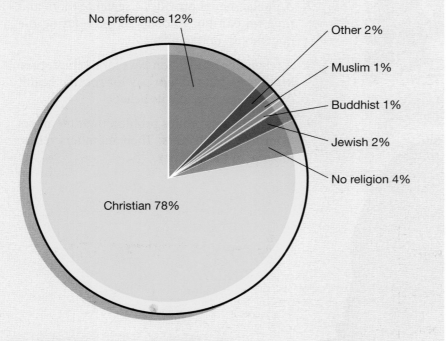

Figure 2.1 Diversity of religions in the United States

These guidelines for the separation of church and state sound simple, but sometimes the First
25 Amendment conflicts with religious practices. The situations below are examples.

1. In a public courtroom, a judge displays the Ten Commandments, a religious document that is important in the Christian and Jewish
30 religions.

2. A Christian prayer is said before a football game at a public school.

3. A Muslim woman covers her head and face in the photograph on her driver's license. It is
35 impossible to identify her in the photograph.

4. A religious organization refuses to hire anyone who does not share its beliefs.

5. Parents from a religious group that prohibits certain medical treatments will not allow their
40 child to have the treatments even though the treatments may save his or her life.

6. In a Native-American religious ceremony, participants eat a local plant that contains an illegal drug.

45 7. A public school provides a separate room and time for Muslim students to pray during the holy month of Ramadan.

8. A religious organization pays for its employees' health care but will not pay for specific health
50 care that goes against its beliefs.

9. Some religious groups prohibit their members from fighting in wars. Their members refuse to serve in the military.

1 Reading for details Ⓡ Ⓦ

> College texts ofen include evidence that supports the main ideas of a topic. Examples, quotations from experts, and/or statistical data are three types of details used as supporting evidence. Learn to read for these details, and be prepared to present details as evidence in class discussions, on writing assignments, or on tests.

A Reread Paragraph 2 of "Separating Religion and Government." Find and underline the sentence that expresses the main idea.

B Circle three examples in the text that support this main idea.

C Compare your answers to Steps A and B in a small group.

2 Writing about numbers Ⓦ

A Look at this chart of words and expressions for numerical data.

Words and Expressions for Numerical Data		
more than less than (just) over (just) under nearly almost about at least approximately	half a quarter a third 50 percent (%) 15 percent (%)	of the population of . . .

B On your own paper, write three sentences that describe the religious diversity in the United States as shown in Figure 2.1. Here is an example:

About 12 percent of the U.S. population has no religious preference.

C Review the graphs in Preparing to Read on page 34. Write two sentences about each graph using the language from the chart in Step A.

3 The Academic Word List Ⓥ

A Review the description of the Academic Word List (AWL) on page 24.

B Look at the AWL words from the text. Match the words with their definitions. Write the letters in the blanks.

_I_ **1.** principle (n)

_D_ **2.** license (n)

_A_ **3.** conflict with (v)

_G_ **4.** impose (v)

_B_ **5.** diverse (adj)

_J_ **6.** identify (v)

_E_ **7.** participant (n)

_C_ **8.** guideline (n)

_H_ **9.** display (v)

_F_ **10.** military (adj)

a. to be in disagreement with

b. including many different kinds

c. information that tells how to do something

d. a document that gives permission to use or own something

e. a person who takes part in an activity

f. related to the armed forces, such as the army or navy

g. to force someone to accept something

h. to show something in an organized way for people to see

i. a rule that explains or controls how something works

j. to recognize or see

4 Applying what you have read Ⓡ

A Reread the examples of conflicts between religious beliefs and the First Amendment at the end of the reading. They are all actual cases that have occurred in the United States. Some cases have already been decided in court; others have not.

B Take turns with a partner explaining how each situation might conflict with the principle of separation of church and state.

C Choose two conflicts from the list that you think have a solution. Explain to your partner how you think each conflict could be resolved. Here is an example:

SITUATION 9: Some religious groups prohibit their members from fighting in wars. Their members refuse to serve in the military.

Conflict: The First Amendment protects people's rights to follow their own religious beliefs. Sometimes military duty conflicts with those beliefs.

Resolution: Their refusal to fight is because of a religious belief; therefore, these people should not have to fight in wars. However, they could serve the country in other ways: in hospitals, parks, and building projects.

D Share your resolution to a conflict you discussed in Step C with the class.

5 Giving reasons Ⓦ Ⓡ

Academic writing often includes the reasons that a situation or an event occurred or existed. Reasons are signaled with connecting words that show cause, such as *because, since, therefore,* and *as a result*. A reason may be provided before or after the event or situation it explains. The order affects the choice of connector as well as the punctuation.

- After: Event/Situation + *because/since* + reason

  *The authors of the Constitution established a system of checks and balances **because** they were worried about abuse of power.*

- Before: *Because/Since* + reason, + event/situation

  ***Because** they were worried about abuse of power, the authors of the Constitution established a system of checks and balances.*

- Before: Reason + *therefore/as a result*, + event/situation

  The authors of the Constitution were worried about abuse of power; therefore, they established a system of checks and balances.

A Read the situations and the reasons for them. Circle the connector that signals the cause. Then underline the reason and double underline the situation or event that it explains. Note if the reason comes before or after the cause.

1. The authors of the Constitution included religious freedom in the First Amendment because they wanted to avoid religious conflicts.

2. The Constitution establishes a policy of "separation of church and state"; therefore, there is no national religion.

3. Because the early settlers were Christian, some Americans think of their country as a Christian nation.

4. Since the Supreme Court has ruled that flag burning is a legal form of political protest, any law that prohibits it is unconstitutional.

B Read the situations below. For each one, write a sentence that gives a reason for the situation. Use connecting words from the box above, and be sure to use correct punctuation.

1. Religious practices and symbols are not permitted on government property, such as courts and public schools.

2. Many people left Europe for the American colonies.

3. The police cannot enter a house without permission from a judge.

4. The police ended the Occupy protests.

Predicting ®

A Look at the title of the text you are going to read. *The right to bear arms* is another way of saying *the right to have firearms*, or guns. You have been reading about the rights guaranteed by the Bill of Rights. Can you predict what the text will say about this right? With a partner, discuss the kind of information you think it will include.

B Look at these pictures of people with guns. Then discuss the questions below in a small group.

   1. Is it easy to buy a gun in the United States?

   2. Do many Americans own guns?

   3. Is gun ownership common in other countries that you are familiar with?

   4. Do you think of the United States as a violent country where people often shoot one another? Explain your answer.

   5. Do you think it is a good idea to allow people to own guns? Why or why not?

Reading 3

GUNS IN AMERICA: THE RIGHT TO BEAR ARMS

The Second Amendment may be the most controversial amendment in the Bill of Rights. To understand it, we must go back in history.

The early Americans had more difficult and dangerous lives than most of us have today. They had to hunt for food and protect themselves from wild animals. There were no police to protect them, so they needed guns for their own defense. There were also conflicts between the settlers and the British army.

Because of these dangers, each colony maintained its own army of citizens, called a *militia,* to protect its residents. The men who wrote the Constitution wanted to be sure that Americans would always be able to protect themselves in this way, so they included the Second Amendment in the Bill of Rights.

Unfortunately, the meaning of the amendment is not clear, and people interpret it in different ways. This is a paraphrase of what it says:

The government should not interfere with the people's right to keep and carry guns because a militia is important for security.

Because the wording is not clear, there are two possible, very different, interpretations. The first one is narrow and the second one is broad:

1. Communities should be permitted to maintain militias, and these militias should carry guns. (Today, *militias* would be the police or the military.)

2. Anyone should be able to own and carry guns. The government must not interfere with this right.

25   The majority of the American population believes that the second interpretation is correct. Between 70 and 80 million Americans own a gun. There are about 300 million firearms in U.S. homes. Laws about owning guns are not the same everywhere. Some states and cities allow people to keep a gun in their homes. Others also allow people
30 to carry guns in public places such as in the street or in a store. Some communities permit some types of guns but prohibit other types.

    Gun ownership is an emotional issue in the United States. Some people believe that gun ownership is a fundamental right; others believe that only the police and the military should carry guns. Every time
35 someone with a gun kills a lot of people, there is public discussion about this issue. In 2012, when a young man in Colorado shot and killed 12 people and wounded 58 others in a crowded movie theater, supporters of **gun control** argued for laws against gun ownership. However, people opposed to gun control reply that if other people in the theater were
40 carrying guns, they could have stopped the young man.

    People on both sides of this issue offer arguments for their views.

gun control laws, policies, and practices that restrict guns

Against gun control	For gun control
A gun ban will not prevent criminals from getting guns.	Guns are a major cause of violence and death.
Citizens should be allowed to own guns for their own protection.	There is a clear relationship between widespread gun ownership and gun violence.
Guns can prevent crimes and save lives.	Guns are used by criminals.
Guns are used for hunting.	Guns often contribute to accidents.
Gun ownership is guaranteed by the Constitution.	Guns can be used against their owners.

1 Scanning ℝ

You will often need to scan when studying for a test or preparing to write an assignment. Scanning a text means reading quickly to find specific information, often facts or statistics. When you scan, you do not read every word. Your eyes pass over the text, stopping only when you find the information you are looking for.

Scan the reading to find the answers to the following questions.

1. What were two dangers that early settlers faced in America?
2. What is the definition of *militia*?
3. Do most Americans believe the narrow or broad interpretation of the Second Amendment?
4. How many guns are in U.S. homes?
5. How many people were killed in the 2012 shooting?

2 Topic sentences Ⓦ

Remember that the topic sentence of a paragraph tells the reader what will be discussed in the rest of the paragraph. It gives the topic and the main point of the paragraph. A good topic sentence should be a general statement, not a statement that is too specific or too emotional.

A Which statement would be the best topic sentence for a paragraph about reasons *against* gun control? Write an *A* (against) next to the statement.

_____ 1. Gun-related deaths are higher in the United States than in any other country.
_____ 2. Americans have strong opinions about gun ownership.
_A_ 3. There are several important reasons why many Americans oppose gun control.
_____ 4. Citizens should be allowed to carry guns for protection against criminals.
_F_ 5. Many Americans think that ordinary people should not own or carry guns.
_____ 6. There is a clear relationship between gun ownership and gun-related deaths.
_____ 7. Gun ownership is guaranteed by the Second Amendment, and no one can take this right away.
_____ 8. Americans love guns.

B Which statement in Step A would be the best topic sentence for a paragraph about reasons *for* gun control? Write an *F* (for) next to the statement. /\ .

C Compare your answers to Steps A and B as a class or in small groups. Explain why the sentences you did not choose are unacceptable topic sentences.

3 Applying what you have read ®

A Read the short newspaper article below. It reports that one man shot another man in self-defense, that is, to protect himself.

HAMPTON, VIRGINIA – A 22-year-old man shot at two attackers early Sunday, killing one of them, a police spokesperson said.

Based on police interviews with witnesses, it appears that the young man was acting in self-defense. He was attending a party at a friend's house. Someone told him that there were people outside who wanted to talk to him.

A witness said that when the young man went outside, two men approached him and started arguing with him.

The two men then jumped on him, knocked him to the ground, and began beating him. The 22-year-old pulled out a gun and fired. A shot hit one of the attackers. The injured man died a few hours later.

B Discuss these questions with a partner or small group.

- How might the incident have ended if the young man did not have a gun?
- Which arguments for and against gun control are relevant to this article? (Review the chart at the end of the text if necessary.)
- Does the incident described in the article make a good argument for the narrow or the broad interpretation of the Second Amendment? Explain.

4 Understanding test questions Ⓐ

When taking a test, it is important for you to understand what kind of information you are expected to give in response to a question. Here are three common types of questions:

Type 1: Simple questions that ask you to identify terms. (They usually ask you to describe *who, what, when, where,* or *how.*)

Type 2: Questions that ask you to explain relationships among ideas and information in the text

Type 3: Questions that ask you to evaluate ideas and information in the text

A Discuss the questions below with a partner and match each question with the correct question type. Write *1*, *2*, or *3* in the blank.

___2___ **a.** What kinds of checks does the judicial branch have on the legislative branch?

___3___ **b.** Why is hate speech sometimes constitutional?

___1___ **c.** What is a militia?

___2___ **d.** What is the difference between the broad and narrow interpretation of the Second Amendment?

___2___ **e.** How does the importance of religion in the United States compare with its importance in Europe?

___3___ **f.** Should burning the flag be against the law? Why or why not?

B Look at the sample answers below. Which question type was most likely asked? Write *1*, *2*, or *3* in the blank.

___2___ **a.** *Religion is important in the lives of many Americans, more important than in the lives of most Europeans. Almost half of all Americans report that they attend weekly religious services. In contrast, just over 20 percent of all French people attend church weekly. An even greater number of Americans report that their religious beliefs are important in their lives. Again, the French report a much lower figure.*

___3___ **b.** *The Supreme Court has ruled that hate speech is constitutional except when it is a threat or when it is likely to cause harm to others. This is an important difference; however, in real situations, it is often difficult to know if words are a threat or if they will lead to violence. Words are threats if people think they are threats. Hate speech may lead to violence indirectly, and we may not know if it was the cause. Because the law is not always clear, it would be better to make hate speech illegal in the United States. It is illegal in many other countries.*

___1___ **c.** *The United States Constitution was adopted in 1789.*

Chapter 2 Academic Vocabulary Review

The following words appear in the readings in Chapter 2. They all come from the Academic Word List, a list of words that researchers have discovered occur frequently in many different types of academic texts. For a complete list of all the Academic Word List words in this chapter and in all the readings in this book, see the Appendix on page 206.

contribute	impose	participate	restrictions
controversial	individuals	principle	security
immigrants	majority	residents	widespread

Complete the following sentences with words from the list above.

1. The _majority_ of Americans support the broad interpretation of the Second Amendment.
2. _Immigrants_ have been coming to the United States from other countries since it became a nation.
3. There is _widespread_ concern about the health of the global economy.
4. The Bill of Rights is not just for citizens; it is for all of the _residents_ in the nation.
5. It is important for all citizens to _participate_ in national elections.
6. The new law is very _controversial._ Many people are arguing about it.
7. There are many different factors that _contribute_ to today's economic problems.
8. The Supreme Court has ruled that there are significant _restrictions_ on freedom of expression.
9. The Bill of Rights establishes a balance between rights of _individuals_ and the power of the government.
10. The police and the military are responsible for the _security_ of the nation.

Practicing Academic Writing

In this unit, you have learned about the rights and freedoms that Americans value so highly. You will write a paragraph based on what you have learned. You will also use what you learned about topic sentences in Developing Writing Skills in Chapter 1.

Individual rights and freedoms

You will write a paragraph about one important right or freedom. Your paragraph will include supporting details that explain why you think this right or freedom is important.

PREPARING TO WRITE

Brainstorming with a group

Brainstorming is a way to get all of your ideas down on paper without using a lot of structure as you do when you make a list or an outline. When you brainstorm with a group, you can increase the number of ideas for your writing. Later you can organize these ideas as you prepare to write. The writing process is not always like a straight line, so save your brainstorming ideas because you may want to return to them when you revise your writing.

A Review the readings in Chapter 2. Think about the topic of the writing assignment as you review them. Which rights and freedoms are most important, and why?

With a small group of classmates, choose two or three rights and freedoms from the list below and brainstorm each one.

- The freedom to express your ideas and opinions even if other people do not like them
- The freedom to practice your religion
- The right to own guns
- The right to talk to a lawyer; to have a fair trial, that is, a speedy and public trial; and to know the charges against you

B List your ideas on the blackboard or a piece of paper. Be sure to include the reasons for your choices. Do not reject anyone's ideas. You don't have to use the ones you don't like.

C Notes from a brainstorming session can be useful, but you need to know how to organize them in order to provide support for your claim. Read these results from an imaginary group brainstorming session about protection against unreasonable searches by the police. (For the moment, ignore the "1" in the first sentence.) With your group, discuss ways you might categorize the ideas:

> **Group B Brainstorming Notes**
>
> Topic: The Right to Protection Against Unreasonable Searches by the Police
>
> __1__ Sometimes the police stop people who turn out to be criminals. The police need to be able search them.
>
> _____ I am afraid of the police. Without this protection, they could come into my house.
>
> _____ A newspaper story said the police put drugs into someone's car during a search and then arrested the owner. That is breaking the law.
>
> _____ Criminals might be hiding things like drugs and guns in their house or car.
>
> _____ What if a police officer is just mad at you and wants to do something bad to you?
>
> _____ It is hard for the police to find criminals if there are too many laws that protect the criminals.
>
> _____ Maybe the police are trying too hard to find criminals, and they break the law, too.

D Now work on your own. Did you notice that the group's ideas generally fall into the three categories below? Go back to the notes in Step C and categorize each idea. Write the number of the category in the blank before each idea. The first one has been done as an example.

1. Reasons why police search homes and cars
2. Reasons why the police might sometimes make unreasonable searches
3. What could happen without protection against unreasonable searches

E Now you are ready to choose a topic for your writing assignment. Choose one of the topics that your group brainstormed in Step A. Skim your notes from the brainstorming session on the right or freedom you chose, and try to find two or three general categories for the ideas, similar to the ones in Step D. Write them below.

_____

_____

F Organize your notes into these categories in the same way you did in Steps C and D.

G Exchange papers with a classmate who chose the same right or freedom. Discuss any questions that you have about the categories you both chose.

Writing first drafts

Your first piece of writing on a topic is a first draft. Very few people write a "perfect" first draft. A first draft gets some ideas, sentences, and paragraphs down on paper that you can then read through and work out how to improve in the next draft.

A Begin your paragraph with a topic sentence about the right or freedom that you have chosen. Remember that a topic sentence

- states what the paragraph will be about;
- makes a claim about the topic that says something important or interesting about the topic.

B Review your brainstorming notes on the topic and your categories.
Find two examples that illustrate the importance of the right or freedom you have chosen.

C Read the sample paragraph below. It is based on the brainstorming notes in Steps C and D of Preparing to Write. Notice that although this topic sentence states the author's opinion, it does not include phrases like *I think* or *I believe*. In academic writing, you don't need to use such phrases. It will be clear that you are expressing your opinion.

Topic sentence

A reason that supports the claim in the topic sentence

First example. It shows a benefit of protection against unreasonable searches.

Second example. It shows a consequence, or what might happen if this protection was not included in the Fourth Amendment.

The protection against unreasonable searches by the police is one of the most important rights guaranteed by the Bill of Rights. This right is part of the Fourth Amendment. The police work very hard to find criminals, so they may sometimes forget about individual rights. That is why the public needs this protection. The police cannot come into your house without a judge's permission and look for some evidence against you. Without the Fourth Amendment, the police could come to your door whenever they wanted and search through your house. That could be very frightening.

D Now write the rest of your paragraph using examples from your notes. Remember to use some of the terms you learned from the readings. Go back to your original brainstorming notes if you need to.

AFTER YOU WRITE

When you have finished your first draft, you can revise and edit it. Revising is the process of improving the content of your writing. You need to check that you have responded correctly to the assignment and expressed yourself clearly. Editing is making the language in the writing accurate (without errors).

A Reread your own paragraph. Check that

- the topic sentence makes a clear claim;
- your paragraph has two examples; and
- you have used terms from the readings.

B Exchange paragraphs with a partner. Discuss the following questions about your paragraphs.

- What right or freedom has your partner chosen?
- Has your partner written a good topic sentence?
- What is the claim in the topic sentence?
- Has your partner explained the right or freedom clearly and correctly?
- Do the examples support your partner's choice? Are they clear?

C Revise your paragraph based on your partner's suggestions or any ideas you had when you were reviewing it.

D Edit your paragraph.

- Read through your paragraph for spelling mistakes, or for grammar mistakes such as subject-verb agreement and verb tense errors.
- Make corrections whenever you find errors.

Unit 2
A Diverse Nation

In this unit, you will look at issues of ethnic diversity in the United States. The term *ethnic diversity* refers to people of different races, cultures, and places of birth. In Chapter 3, you will focus on the historical background of ethnic diversity in the United States. You will also examine the challenges and hardships of native people, slaves, and immigrants. In Chapter 4, you will look at diversity today, including the reasons for the continued arrival of immigrants, both legal and illegal.

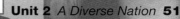

Contents

In Unit 2, you will read and write about the following topics.

Skills

In Unit 2, you will practice the following skills.

(R) Reading Skills	**(W) Writing Skills**
Examining graphics Previewing art Reading for main ideas Reading for details Applying what you have read Thinking about the topic Reading boxed texts Predicting Scanning Increasing reading speed Reading actively Understanding cartoons	The passive voice Writing descriptions Writing about growth
(V) Vocabulary Skills	**(A) Academic Success Skills**
Words related to the topic Synonyms Guessing meaning from context Suffixes Words related to the topic Using a dictionary	Highlighting Taking notes with a chart Answering true/false questions Taking notes in an outline

Learning Outcomes

Write two paragraphs about contrasting attitudes toward diversity

Previewing the Unit

Before reading a unit (or chapter) in a textbook, it is a good idea to preview the contents page and think about the topics that will be covered. This will help you understand how the unit is organized and what it is going to be about.

Read the contents page for Unit 2 on page 52 and do the following activities.

Chapter 3: The Origins of Diversity

This chapter explores the history and experiences of these important groups: Native Americans who lived on the land before European settlers arrived, slaves brought to the country from Africa, and immigrants who arrived in large numbers in the nineteenth and twentieth centuries. Discuss the following questions with a partner or small group.

1. We often think of North America as almost empty when the settlers arrived. What do you think the size of the native population was, compared with the number of settlers?
2. Before the middle of the twentieth century, which countries did the largest number of immigrants to the United States come from?
3. Read the quotation below. What does it mean?

> Every American has the soul of an immigrant.
> – Jim Sheridan, Irish film director

Chapter 4: Diversity in Today's United States

This chapter focuses on the diversity of the U.S. population today, in particular on the largest immigrant groups, Latinos and Asian Americans. It also explores the issue of illegal immigration. Examine the picture on page 78. Then discuss these questions with your partner or group.

1. Which countries do you think most immigrants to the United States come from today? Why is this different from the nineteenth and early twentieth centuries?
2. What challenges do today's immigrants have when they arrive? Are they the same or different from the challenges of earlier immigrants?
3. What special problems do minorities face, that is, people who are not from a white European background?
4. Immigrants can become American citizens, but do you think they all become "American"?

Chapter 3
The Origins of Diversity

1 Examining graphics ®

With your partner or group, look at the maps below and discuss this question:
What will the reading "America's First People" be about?

Land transferred from Native American (Indian) to white ownership (1784–1880)

Native American lands are shown in green.

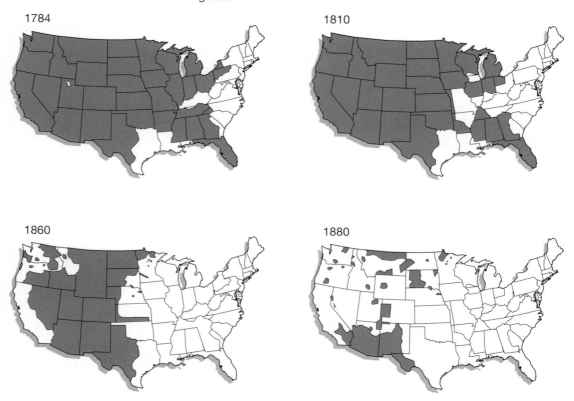

1784   1810

1860   1880

Source: **Sam Hilliard, Louisiana State University**

2 Previewing art ®

Look at the photographs on page 57 and discuss these questions with a partner.

1. What might have happened to these children after entering the Carlisle School?

2. What do the photographs and the maps above have in common?

Reading 1

AMERICA'S FIRST PEOPLE

Early contact between settlers and native people

When European settlers arrived in North America at the end of the fifteenth century, there were approximately 10 million native people who spoke over 300 different languages. The first Europeans believed they had landed in India, so they called the native people *Indians*.
5 Indian and European cultures were very different, and the two groups often had problems understanding each other. Indian communities stretched from one end of North America to the other, and they all had their own characteristics. Many were nomads who moved across the land to hunt. Like all Indian communities, they had a deep respect
10 for the natural world. They believed that if they took care of the land, they could use it to live on and to hunt; they did not own land in the European way. In contrast, the settlers built homes and towns, bought and sold land, and wanted to own land.

Relations between Indians and Europeans ranged from
15 cooperation to violent conflict. At first, the European settlers often depended on the Indians for assistance and trade. As the number of settlers increased, however, they began to move farther into Indian territory, and conflicts became more frequent and more violent. There was death and destruction on both sides, but native people were
20 usually the losers in these struggles for control of the land.

Many Indian communities were destroyed by the actions of the settlers and later on by the policies of the new American government. When the Europeans first arrived, they brought new diseases, such as measles and smallpox, which killed huge numbers of Indians. As
25 more settlers came and wanted the rich land that the various groups of Indians, or tribes, lived on, battles began between the government and various tribes for this land.

Indian territory
a part of the country where many Native Americans lived

Loss of Indian land

Indian tribes occupied the entire country when the settlers first arrived. By 1880, they had lost nearly all of it. Starting in 1778, the United States government made hundreds of treaties, or written agreements, with native tribes in order to provide more space for the settlers. Indians gave up their rights to their territory in exchange for food, money, and, perhaps most importantly, the government's promise to leave them in peace. Sometimes a tribe was allowed to stay on a small part of its original land. This small area was called a **reservation.** In other cases, the tribe simply moved west. This was the beginning of the loss of Indian land.

Most European Americans in the eighteenth and nineteenth centuries believed that whites were superior to Indians. President Andrew Jackson described native people as children who needed his guidance and protection. He, as well as many other Americans, believed the treaties were good for the Indians because they allowed native people to live in peace, separate from whites. Unfortunately, the government often did not keep the promises in these treaties. As the country continued to grow, settlers needed still more land, including the land that the government had given to the native tribes in treaties. The government broke its promises to the Indians and began a policy of removal, that is, pushing more and more native people farther west or onto reservations.

In 1830, Congress passed the Removal Act. This law required native tribes to leave their land and settle in Indian Territory, west of the Mississippi River. Some tribes refused to go, particularly the Cherokee. So in 1838, thousands of soldiers and volunteers forced the Cherokee to leave their homes. Hundreds of them were beaten, imprisoned, or murdered. Those who survived were forced to travel 1,000 miles to the Indian Territory, with little food, water, or protection. Approximately 4,000 Cherokee died on this journey, which has been called the *Trail of Tears.*

reservation an area of land set aside by the U.S. government for native people

"The Trail of Tears" by Robert Lindneux

Native culture

Another factor that had a negative effect on native culture was the
60 government's education policy. The federal government's goal for
Indian education from the 1880s through the 1920s was the assimilation
of native children into white American culture. Assimilation means
that a group learns and uses the customs and culture of a different
group. Many native children were required to leave their families and
65 attend government **boarding schools**. The children lived at these
schools, where their traditional ways were replaced by the customs
and behavior of white Americans. The government hoped that these
children would learn the language, values, and culture of white
American society. This policy of assimilation was partly successful.
70 It is estimated that more than two-thirds of the original 300 native
languages are dead or dying. Only a few have more than 5,000
speakers.

boarding school
a school where
students live and
attend classes

Children as they arrived at the Carlisle school

Children after arriving at
the Carlisle school

Today, native cultures are making a comeback. In 1900, the
population had dropped to about 250,000, but it grew rapidly in the
75 twentieth century. On the 2010 **census**, 5.2 million people reported
that they were *Native American*.* This was a 39 percent increase since
the 2000 census. The Cherokee and Navajo nations have the largest
populations. On reservations, tribes now have their own form of
government, tribal courts, and police. Many Native Americans are
80 working to preserve their cultural heritage, including their tribal
languages.

census the
official count of the
population size

---

* This new term originated in the twentieth century. Many native people now
use the term Native American, while others prefer the older term, Indian.

1 Reading for main ideas Ⓡ

Check (✓) the sentence that best states the main idea of the reading.

_____ **1.** Native American communities are recovering from past challenges.

_____ **2.** Government policies and attitudes of white Americans seriously damaged or destroyed many native communities.

_____ **3.** European American settlers pushed native peoples off their land and onto special reservations.

2 Reading for details Ⓡ Ⓐ

Once you have identified a main idea, remember that it is important to look for details that support it. One way to do this is to identify key terms or points. For example, to find details that support this main idea, you would look for information in the text about "unpopular and offensive ideas."

Freedom of speech is broad enough to protect **unpopular and offensive ideas**.

Details can be facts, statistics, examples, anecdotes, or other types of information. Reading for details helps you understand the reading and can also help you prepare for a test.

- Find the main idea of the reading and mark key terms or key points.
- Find details that explain key terms or support key points.

A Review the sentence that you chose in Task 1.

B Compare your choice with a partner. If you are unsure of the right answer, check with your teacher.

C Circle the key terms and key points in the statement that you chose. Then reread the text for details that explain these terms or support these points. Underline them.

D Listing details in a chart can help you remember them. Write the key terms or key points from Step C in the headings of the chart below. The first term has been filled in for you. Then complete the chart with the details you underlined in the text in Step C.

Key term/point 1: Government policies	Key term/point 2:	Key term/point 3:

3 The passive voice Ⓦ

> The passive form of the verb (*be* + past participle) is common in academic writing, so it is important to be able to recognize and use this form.
>
> The passive is a good choice if any of these, or a combination of these, are true:
>
> - The writer wants to focus on the person or thing being acted upon.
> - The performer of the action is unknown.
> - The performer of the action is unimportant.
>
> Here are some examples of the passive:
>
> The Constitution **was adopted** in 1789.
> Religious freedom **is guaranteed** by the First Amendment.

A Underline the passive verb form in each sentence from the text below.

1. Many native communities were almost destroyed by the actions of the settlers and the policies of the American government.
2. Sometimes a tribe was allowed to stay on a small part of its original land.
3. Hundreds of Cherokee were beaten, imprisoned, or murdered.
4. The Cherokee who survived were forced to march 1,000 miles.

B Find two more examples of the passive voice in Paragraph 7. Underline them.

C Work with a partner. Complete each sentence with the correct active or passive form of the verb. Circle your choices and discuss your reasons for them.

1. The long journey of the Cherokee (*called / is called*) the Trail of Tears.
2. Many Cherokee (*imprisoned or killed / were imprisoned or killed*) when they would not leave their land.
3. The United States government (*broke / was broken*) many of its treaties with native tribes.
4. Native tribes (*forced / were forced*) to move west of the Mississippi River.
5. Competition for land (*created / was created*) conflict between the Europeans and native people.

D Write a sentence about Native Americans that is not in the text. Use the passive voice.

Native Americans _____ .

4 Applying what you have read Ⓡ

Many people, both from the United States and other countries, get their ideas about the first people of America from movies. Discuss the following questions about the image of or stereotype of Native Americans as a class:

- What have you seen about Native Americans in movies?
- How does what you have seen in movies compare with the information in the reading?

1 Words related to the topic Ⓥ

> Understanding important words and ideas about a topic before you read helps to build your background knowledge. This can help you read more effectively.

A Study the definitions.

> **slave:** *a person who is legally owned by someone else and has to work for him or her*
>
> **negro:** *a person of African origin with dark skin. This term was used during the nineteenth and early twentieth centuries but is now considered negative.*
>
> **auction:** *a public sale of property, where people offer more and more money for each piece of property, until it is sold to the person who will pay most*

B Discuss these questions with a partner.

1. Have you been to an auction? Describe your experience.
2. What kinds of things are bought and sold at an auction?

2 Thinking about the topic Ⓡ

A Look at the signs below.

B With a partner, discuss what you think happened at slave auctions.

1. Who attended slave auctions?
2. Who bought slaves?
3. How were slaves treated?

Reading 2

SLAVERY

The economics of slavery

The work of slaves was essential to the agricultural economy of the southern United States, especially for growing cotton. Growing cotton required a large number of workers. For cotton farmers, slave labor was an answer to this problem. However, the economic importance of
5 slavery went beyond the South. Africans, who were taken from their villages, were loaded onto ships that were owned by businessmen from all over the United States and Europe. The ships sailed to ports in the Caribbean Islands and the southern United States, where the Africans were sold as slaves. In the Caribbean ports, the ships picked
10 up molasses, a raw syrup made from Caribbean sugar, and brought it to northern cities such as Boston and New York. The molasses was then made into rum, an alcoholic drink. Some of the rum was shipped to Africa and traded for slaves. The slaves were then shipped to the Caribbean, and the cycle began again. This process was called
15 *Triangular Trade* because the path formed a large triangle that stretched across the Atlantic Ocean (see Figure 3.1). The cotton was shipped to factories in the northern United States and in Great Britain, where it was made into cloth and sold all over the world.

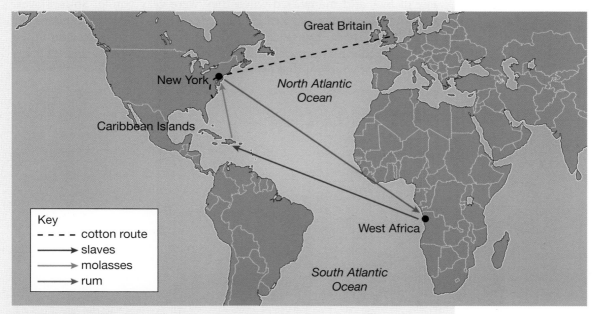

Figure 3.1 Triangular Trade

From the sixteenth to the nineteenth centuries, about 12 million
20 Africans were sent to the New World (North and South America) as slaves. Only about 5 percent of them came to the United States. In spite of the importance of the slave trade, many Americans opposed it.

In 1807, the U.S. Congress passed a law that prohibited people from importing slaves. However, owning slaves remained legal in many states. Everyone profited from slavery – the cotton farmers, the cloth factory owners, the rum producers, the slave traders, the ship owners, and people who bought cotton cloth – everyone except, of course, the slaves themselves.

The lives of slaves

Unlike most of the people who have come to America, these Africans were brought against their will. Many of them died either in Africa before the journey or during the journey across the Atlantic Ocean, which lasted about seven weeks. The conditions on ships were dreadful; the passengers were often chained side by side, with no space to move. Experts estimate that between 10 and 25 percent of the slaves died on the journey. The ones who survived were sold. Husbands and wives, children and parents were often separated. They became the property of the people who bought them, with no rights of their own. They had to work long hours; most worked in the cotton fields, up to 16 hours a day during the harvest. They received poor food, and rough clothing and housing. If they disobeyed orders or tried to escape, the punishment was severe and painful. Women had to work until childbirth and return to work immediately afterward. Children began working at the age of five, and many died when they were very young. Some slaves, especially those who worked inside their owners' houses, lived in better conditions. These "house slaves" still had hard lives, however, and they had no freedom. The average life of a slave was very short – just 22 years – half that of whites at that time.

The end of slavery

The slaves received their freedom at the end of the American Civil War (1861–1865), which divided the North and the South. Disagreement
50 about slavery was one of the major causes of the war. The South wanted to preserve slavery; it was essential to their prosperity. The North wanted to end it. In 1863, President Lincoln's Emancipation Proclamation ended slavery in the South. The North won the war, and in 1865, the Thirteenth Amendment to the Constitution made slavery illegal.

Slave Narratives

After the end of slavery, some slaves began to tell their stories. Here is part of one of these slave narratives. This narrative is from an interview with a slave named Fountain Hughes. It is written just the way Hughes spoke.

. . . Now I couldn't go from here across the street, or I couldn't go to nobody's house without a note, or something from my master. Whoever he sent me to, they would give me another pass and I'd bring that back . . . to show how long I'd been gone. We couldn't go out and stay an hour or two hours or something like that. . . . I couldn't just walk away like the people do now, you know. We were slaves. We belonged to people. They'd sell us like they sell horses and cows and hogs and all like that. They'd have an auction bench, and they'd put you on, up on the bench and bid on you just same as bidding on cattle.

1 Highlighting Ⓐ

One way to remember what you have read is to highlight important information. This can help you study for a test on the material. Use these guidelines for highlighting text:

- Highlight the main idea(s)
- Highlight key facts and details
- Do not highlight minor details or less important information
- Try to highlight phrases and terms instead of entire sentences
- Do not highlight many sentences or too much of the text

A Read this paragraph from the text and highlight the most important information about the lives of slaves. One example has been done for you.

Unlike most of the people who have come to America, these Africans were brought against their will. Many of them died either in Africa before the journey or during the journey across the Atlantic Ocean, which lasted about seven weeks. The conditions on ships were dreadful; the passengers were often chained side by side, with no space to move. Experts estimate that between 10 and 25 percent of the slaves died on the journey. The ones who survived were sold. Husbands and wives, children and parents were often separated. They became the property of the people who bought them, with no rights of their own. They had to work long hours; most worked in the cotton fields, up to 16 hours a day during the harvest. They received poor food, and rough clothing and housing. If they disobeyed orders or tried to escape, the punishment was severe and painful. Women had to work until childbirth and return to work immediately afterward. Children began working at the age of five, and many died when they were very young. Some slaves, especially those who worked inside their owners' houses, lived in better conditions. These "house slaves" still had hard lives, however, and they had no freedom. The average life of a slave was very short – just 22 years – half that of whites at that time.

B Compare your work with a classmate's. If you have highlighted different information, explain why you think your information is important.

C Now go back to the text. The reading claims that slavery was one of the major causes of the Civil War. Highlight parts of the text that support this claim.

2 Examining graphics ®

> Graphics are charts, maps, or tables that are often used to expand on information in a reading. You can usually find information more quickly and easily in a graphic than in the text.

A Use the information in the map on page 61 to fill in the chart.

	Where picked up?	Where shipped to?
Slaves		
Molasses		
Rum		
Cotton		

Work with a partner to complete the following activities.

B Discuss these questions.

1. How is all of the information in the chart in Step A related?
2. How does the map expand on information in the reading?
3. Does the map help you understand the economics of slavery? If so, in what way?

3 Synonyms Ⓥ

There are many words that can say the same thing, for example, about an idea, an event, or a group of people. Different words with similar meanings are called *synonyms*. You may already know many common descriptive words. In academic texts, however, writers often use synonyms that are less common words. When you write, do as writers do. Try to vary your language and use less common synonyms.

A Find synonyms for these common words and phrases in the text (including the boxed text). Look for words that have similar meaning but are less common. Write the synonyms in the blanks. The line number appears after each word.

1. very important   _____ (Line 1)
2. work (*n*)   _____ (Line 3)
3. were against   _____ (Line 22)
4. made money   _____ (Line 25)
5. makers   _____ (Line 26)
6. very bad   _____ (Line 32)
7. didn't follow   _____ (Line 40)
8. keep   _____ (Line 51)
9. economic success   _____ (Line 51)
10. stories   _____ (Line 3 of the boxed text)

B Compare your answers with a partner.

4 Reading boxed texts Ⓡ

Boxed texts are sometimes used to display primary texts. Primary texts are original documents. Learning to understand boxed texts is an important part of academic study.

A Reread the boxed text at the end of the reading. Note the kinds of information it includes.

B List the kinds of information that Fountain Hughes gives.

C In a small group, compare your lists from Step B. Discuss the differences between the primary text in the boxed text on page 63 and the main text. What can you learn from the boxed text that you cannot learn from the main text?

5 The passive voice Ⓦ

> The passive is often used to describe a process. In describing a process, key terms can be repeated sentence to sentence to connect the ideas and to create a "chain" of events.
>
> In the example below, the passive is used to describe the steps or process of getting cotton from farms to merchant ships. The chain begins with the key word *cotton* toward the end of the first sentence. *Cotton* then appears at the beginning of the next sentence, which is in the passive. The key words are in **bold** and the passive form of the verb is underlined.

The slaves did the most difficult work; they picked the raw **cotton** from the fields. The raw **cotton** was fed into a machine called a *cotton gin*, which separated the seeds from the cotton fibers, which are called **lint**. Then the **lint** was packed into **bales** that weighed 500 pounds or more. These **bales** were carried in wagons to seaports, where ships waited to take them to factories in Great Britain.

A The description of Triangular Trade below is also an example of a text chain. Circle the three key words that are repeated. Underline the passive forms of the verb.

In the Caribbean ports, the ships picked up molasses, a syrup from Caribbean sugar, and brought it to northern cities such as Boston and New York. The molasses was then made into rum, an alcoholic drink. Some of the rum was shipped to Africa and traded for slaves. The slaves were then shipped to the Caribbean, and the cycle began again.

B Go back to Step A. Draw arrows between the key words that you circled. Note the passive verb that you underlined. Look at the example in the box again if necessary.

C Read each sentence below. Then add a second sentence to create a two-sentence text chain.

1. In factories in England, the cotton was woven into cloth.

_____

2. The sugar was cooked and made into molasses.

_____

3. The ships that returned to the ports in the Caribbean were filled with slaves.

_____

1 Predicting Ⓡ

It is a good habit to try to predict the information in a text before you read it. You can often predict the general content of a text by looking at the headings, graphics, and the first sentence of each paragraph.

A Quickly read the following parts of "A Country of Immigrants."

- The graph
- The headings
- The first sentence of each paragraph

B In a small group, discuss what you think this reading will be about.

2 Thinking about the topic Ⓡ

A Look at the photographs of immigrants to the United States.

B For each photograph, discuss the following questions in a group.

1. When did these people come to the United States? How do you know?
2. Why do you think they came?
3. Do the people in the photographs have anything in common?
4. Do you know of people who immigrated to another country at the same time as the immigrants in the photographs? Why did they immigrate?

Reading 3

A COUNTRY OF IMMIGRANTS

A flood of newcomers

The United States is a country of immigrants. It has received more immigrants than any other nation in modern history. In the seventeenth and eighteenth centuries, most of the immigrants to the American colonies came from western Europe, primarily England,
5 Scotland, Ireland, the Netherlands, and Germany. Some were looking for adventure; some wanted cheap land to farm. Others were escaping wars, revolutions, or religious persecution. However, most of them were simply poor people hoping for better economic opportunities.

In the beginning of the nineteenth century, shorter travel time and
10 cheaper fares made the voyage easier. This allowed more people to immigrate. From 1820 to 1875, about 7 million newcomers entered the United States, but the greatest numbers came between 1875 and 1920. During this period, about 24 million immigrants poured into the United States from almost every part of the world, reaching a
15 peak in the first 10 years of the twentieth century. At this time, the United States needed lots of workers and farmers, so the government encouraged immigration. Immigrant labor was a major factor in the country's economic prosperity. However, this flood of immigrants began to alarm many American citizens. They believed that the
20 immigrants, who worked for low wages, were taking their jobs away. Just as importantly, many of them believed that the large number of immigrants threatened the nation's identity. During the mid-1800s, some Americans began to demand laws to make it harder for people to immigrate to the United States.

Discrimination against immigrants

25 Most immigrants had difficult lives, but two immigrant groups who faced particular hardships in the second half of the nineteenth century were the Chinese and the Irish. Many Chinese came as miners when gold was discovered in California in 1849. Often, they were treated badly by other miners; some were the victims of violence.
30 The government did not do much to protect them. In addition, more than 12,000 Chinese immigrants worked on the construction of the Transcontinental Railroad. This was a huge project that connected the middle of the country to California by railroad. The Chinese did the most dangerous work, yet they would work for lower pay than
35 white workers. This made white workers angry. Americans also found Chinese customs strange and foreign. The Chinese often became the victims of discrimination; in other words, they could be treated badly just because they were Chinese.

On the East Coast, one of the largest groups of immigrants was the
40 Irish. Between 1846 and 1880, nearly 2 million people arrived from

Ireland. Most were escaping terrible economic conditions in Ireland, yet when they arrived in the United States, they also faced difficult conditions. Many immigrants were sick and weak after the long, hard journey. Living conditions were crowded, often with as many as 10 people sleeping in one room. Because so many new immigrants arrived at the same time, they could not all find jobs. When they found work, it was difficult and sometimes dangerous, and the pay was low. Men took jobs building homes and bridges, and cleaning streets. Women worked as servants in American homes, or they worked in factories sewing clothes up to 14 hours a day. As with the Chinese, many Americans believed the Irish were taking away their jobs, and as a result, they, too, often faced hostility. In addition, many Americans were prejudiced against the Irish because of their religion, Catholicism.

Figure 3.2 Immigration to the United States 1831–1930 (in thousands)

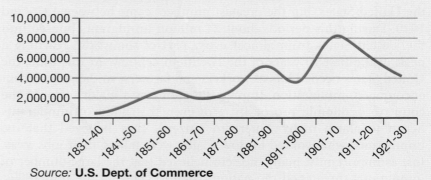

Source: **U.S. Dept. of Commerce**

Restrictions on immigration

Competition for jobs was a source of conflict between American citizens and many immigrants but not the only one. Some Americans also believed that the large number of immigrants was a burden for the rest of the population because they needed government services: schools, running water, and police protection. There were also many misunderstandings between Americans and the new immigrants based on cultural differences. In response to fears about the flood of newcomers, Congress passed a law to limit immigration. It allowed only immigrants who could read and write. It also prohibited all immigration from Asia. In 1921, Congress established a system of quotas. Under the quota system, limits on immigration from each country were based on the number of people from that country in the United States in 1920. Quotas were only for white immigrants; nonwhite immigrants were prohibited from entering the country at that time. This quota system, which favored immigrants from Europe, ended in 1965.

Each new group of immigrants that comes to the United States faces its own challenges. Latinos, Asians, and Africans are the immigrants whose appearance and culture differ the most from the majority, that is, white Americans of European background. They are the immigrants who most frequently face anti-immigrant hostility and discrimination. Often the reasons are the same as they have been throughout history: competition for jobs and resources as well as misunderstanding of new and different cultures.

The Mariel Boatlift

South Florida has been home to many Cuban Americans since the Communists came to power in Cuba in 1959. Many Cubans immigrated at that time, but soon after that, it became more difficult for people to leave the island – except for a brief period in 1980. As part of an agreement between the United States and Cuba, Cubans were suddenly allowed to sail out of Mariel Harbor. A flood of 125,000 Cubans crossed the hundred miles of ocean to the tip of Florida in small boats. Just as suddenly, six months later, it ended when Castro closed the harbor.

1 Taking notes with a chart Ⓐ

A Look at the chart below. It is organized to show three themes in the history of immigration to the United States.

Pushes are reasons why people chose to leave their countries.

Pulls are reasons why people chose to come to the United States.

Barriers are things that the U.S. government or citizens have done in order to stop or slow immigration.

Pushes	Pulls	Barriers
religious persecution in Europe		

B Make a chart like the one above on a separate piece of paper. Fill it in with information from the text. One piece of information is filled in as an example.

C Compare your chart with a partner's.

2 Guessing meaning from context Ⓥ

Sometimes you can guess the meaning of a word from its *context*, that is, the words and sentences surrounding the word. The context can give clues, such as whether the word means something positive (good) or something negative (bad).

A The word *persecution* (Line 7) is probably a new word for you. Study this example. It explains how clues in the text indicate the meaning of *persecution*.

Some were looking for adventure; some wanted cheap land to farm. Others were escaping wars, revolutions, or religious **persecution**.

Is *persecution* positive or negative? The word *escaping* suggests that it is negative. Why would people need to escape because of their religion? Perhaps the immigrants did not like the religion in their old country. Or, perhaps the old country did not like the religion of the immigrants. In either case, *persecution* means "bad treatment." In other words, the immigrants were treated badly because of their religion.

B Read the sentences from the text. Use the context to understand the meanings of the words in **bold**. First, decide if the bolded word is positive or negative, and write *P* or *N* in the blank. Then underline the word or words in the context that helped you decide.

_____ **1.** However, this flood of immigrants began to **alarm** many American citizens. They believed that the immigrants, who worked for low wages, were taking their jobs.

_____ **2.** Most immigrants had difficult lives, but two immigrant groups who faced particular **hardships** in the second half of the nineteenth century were the Chinese and the Irish.

_____ **3.** As they had with the Chinese, many Americans believed the Irish were taking away their jobs and as a result, the Irish, too, often faced **hostility**.

_____ **4.** Quotas were only for white immigrants; nonwhite immigrants were prohibited from entering the country at that time. This quota system, which **favored** immigrants from Europe, ended in 1965.

C Compare your answers to Step B as a class.

3 Examining graphics ®

Charts and tables provide important facts that add to the information in the text. Reading charts and tables and connecting the ideas in them to ideas in the text can deepen your understanding of academic material.

A Look back at Figure 3.2 and answer the questions below.

1. During which 10-year period did immigration reach the highest point? _____

2. Did immigration remain at this high level? _____

B Now go back to the text. Find the parts that support your answers to Step A. Underline them.

4 Scanning ®

Scanning is looking quickly through a text to find information, such as a name, date, or definition. When you scan, you do not read every word. Your eyes pass over the text, stopping only when you find the word or information you are looking for. You may need to do this when preparing for a test or a writing assignment.

Scan the text, including the boxed text, to find the answers to the questions.

1. How many immigrants came to the United States between 1875 and 1920? _____

2. What two kinds of work did most Chinese immigrants do? _____ , _____

3. When did Congress establish a quota system for immigration? _____

4. When did the quota system end?_____

5. Where did immigrants in the Mariel Boatlift come from? _____

Chapter 3 Academic Vocabulary Review

The following words appear in the readings in Chapter 3. They all come from the Academic Word List, a list of words that researchers have discovered occur frequently in many different types of academic texts. For a complete list of all the Academic Word List words in this chapter and in all the readings in this book, see the Appendix on page 206.

challenge	cycles	policy	resources
construction	estimate (v)	primarily	survived
cooperation	identity	range	volunteers

Complete the following sentences with words from the list above.

1. During the first century of U.S. history, Americans began to develop a strong sense of national _____ .

2. After the earthquake, the police and military searched for people who _____ .

3. The economy often goes in _____ . It is strong for a period, then weak, and then strong again.

4. U.S. immigration _____ has changed a great deal in U.S. history. At first, it was very open, but later, it placed limits on who could enter the country.

5. Although immigrants in the nineteenth century entered the country _____ through New York, some entered through California or crossed the Mexican border into Texas.

6. Many immigrants worked on the _____ of roads, railways, and subways.

7. States sometimes ask the federal government for help because they do not have enough _____ to help new immigrants.

8. Competition for jobs among immigrant groups was common, but there was also a great deal of _____ among immigrant communities.

9. Experts _____ the number of immigrants who will come to the United States every year.

10. The first _____ that many immigrants face is learning English.

Developing Writing Skills

In this section, you will learn writing strategies for using information from texts that you have read. You will use charts to help you. You will not write a paragraph, but you will do all of the preparation for it. You will also use what you learn here to complete the writing assignment at the end of this unit.

Expressing ideas in your own words

One of the biggest challenges in academic writing is finding your own words to express ideas that you have read about. Students often want to use the exact words from the text because they think it is the best way to express these ideas. However, it is not acceptable in academic writing to use someone else's ideas as if they were yours. You must present ideas in your own words. Here are some guidelines to help you. It is a good practice to follow these steps every time you read an assignment.

1. Highlight important ideas and details.
2. Take notes on a separate piece of paper.
3. Do not copy sentences from the text. Use your own words to restate what is in the reading.
4. When you begin writing, refer only to your notes, not to the original text.

A In this chapter, you learned about the struggles and journeys of Native Americans, enslaved Africans, and immigrants. Although the experiences of these people were very different, all of them faced many hardships. Think about the differences and similarities of the experiences of these three groups of people.

B Make notes to prepare for the following writing assignment:

Describe the ways in which hardships were similar or different across the three groups.

Begin by reviewing all three texts. Highlight the parts that are relevant to the assignment. Remember: Highlight only the most important facts and ideas.

C Review the chart below. The first column lists categories of challenges and hardships that the three groups faced. Study these categories and review the material that you highlighted in the texts.

	Native Americans	Enslaved Africans	Immigrants
Government laws and policies			
Working conditions			
Physical violence and mistreatment			
Cultural differences			
Attitudes of other groups			
Other			

D Now make a chart like the one in Step C. Use a whole page to have plenty of room to write in the boxes.

- Fill in the chart with examples of hardship. Use the information that you highlighted in the readings. For some rows, you may have more than one piece of information; for others, you may have nothing.
- Be sure to include details or examples for each group.
- Write short notes and phrases, not whole sentences.
- Be sure to use your own words.

E In a small group, discuss the information in your charts. Then add information and ideas from the discussion to your chart.

F Now use your chart to decide what to write about. Choose two types of hardships. Be sure to choose categories with details and examples for at least two groups.

G Get ready to state the first type of hardship. Look at these example sentences:

One hardship that they faced was . . .
Physical violence against the . . . was . . .
. . . caused problems for many of the groups.
It was very difficult for . . . because . . .

Now state the first type of hardship. Do not look at the texts. Use your own words.

1. _____

Give a specific example of this hardship for each of your groups. Use the information from your chart.

a. _____

b. _____

c. _____

H Next, state the second type of hardship. Do not look at the texts. Use your own words. You can use the models in Step G.

2. _____

Give a specific example of this hardship for each of your groups. Use the notes from your chart to help you.

a. _____

b. _____

c. _____

I Look back at the highlighted sentences in the texts that are related to your sentences. Compare them. Explain the differences to a classmate.

Chapter 4
Diversity in Today's United States

PREPARING TO READ

1 Increasing reading speed ®

> Academic courses often require quite a lot of reading, but you will not always have time to read every text slowly and carefully. Reading speed can be as important as comprehension, especially in timed tests. Here are some strategies for increasing your reading speed.
>
> - Read the text straight through.
> - Try not to go over the text again and again.
> - Guess at the general meaning of words that you do not know.
> - Skip over words that you do not know and that do not seem very important.
> - Slow down slightly for key information, such as definitions and main ideas.

A Read the text "America's Increasing Diversity." Use the strategies listed above. For this task, do not read the table or boxed text.

1. Before you begin, enter your starting time: _____

2. After you finish, enter your finishing time: _____

B Calculate your reading speed.

Number of words in the text (614) ÷

Number of minutes it took you to read the text = your Reading Speed

Reading speed: _____

Your goal should be about 150–180 words per minute.

C Check your reading comprehension. Answer these questions. Do not look at the text.

1. In what way are immigration patterns today different from earlier patterns?

2. What group is in the majority in the United States?

3. Why do some people oppose continued high rates of immigration?

2 Examining graphics ®

A Find evidence in Figure 4.1 on page 79 for your answer to question 1 in Step C above. Underline it.

B Compare your answer to a classmate's answer.

Reading 1

AMERICA'S INCREASING DIVERSITY

The 2010 census shows that the United States is more racially and
ethnically diverse than at any time in its history. School districts in
big cities report that they serve immigrant children from all over
the world speaking more than a hundred different languages. Today,
5 however, immigrants do not just go to the traditional immigrant cities
on the coasts, like New York, Miami, Los Angeles, and San Francisco.
They also go to the suburbs and to smaller towns and cities in states
like Georgia, Iowa, Colorado, and North Carolina.

This growing diversity is partly the result of a change in
10 immigration policy. A 1965 immigration law made it easier to
immigrate from places other than Europe. Since that time, there has
been a sharp increase in immigration from Latin America and Asia.
Currently, the largest number of immigrants come from Mexico,
followed by China, India, and the Philippines (see Figure 4.1).

A new immigrant arrives in the United States every 30
seconds, and approximately 12 percent of the people now
living in the United States were born in another country.
Although this is higher than 35 years ago, when the
percentage was about 5, it is lower than during the first
20 decades of the twentieth century, when it was closer to 15
percent.

In the decade between 2000 and 2010, the U.S.
population grew by more than 27 million. Nonwhites
accounted for more than 90 percent of this growth.
25 Immigration contributed significantly to this development,
but birthrates are also an important factor. For the first
time, in 2012, more nonwhite babies were born in the
United States than white babies. Whites have become
a minority in five states and in many major cities, including
30 Houston, Las Vegas, Los Angeles, Miami, Memphis, New
York, and the nation's capital, Washington, D.C.

The white population (non-Latino) is the majority at
about 63 percent; the African American population has
remained stable at about 13 percent. The big changes have
35 been in the increases in Latino and Asian American
populations. These populations have affected the way
the country looks, feels, and sounds. The popularity of
Latino stars like Jennifer Lopez and Selena Gomez has spread across
the entire country. In 2011, there were 84 international team members
40 playing for the National Basketball Association, including the popular
Chinese player, Yao Ming, of the Houston Rockets. Mexican tacos
are becoming as popular as hot dogs, Korean kimchi is appearing
on hamburgers instead of pickles, and Americans are eating more
salsa than ketchup.

45 Although America is a country of immigrants, many Americans
have had mixed feelings about new immigrants, and this is still true
today. Critics strongly oppose the continued high immigration rate.
Some claim that immigrants take jobs away from Americans and keep
wages low. It is sometimes also argued that immigrants use too many
50 expensive public resources, such as medical services and schools,
and that immigrants do not want to learn English or become part of
American culture.

However, there are many supporters of immigration in the United
State and many Americans who have very positive feelings about
55 immigrants. Supporters of immigration argue that the country needs
immigrants. They point out that many of the people working in **high-
tech** companies are immigrants. Some of the country's most familiar
Internet businesses, such as Google, Intel, and eBay, were started by
people from other countries.

Figure 4.1
Legal immigration to the United States by country
of origin in 2011

Country	Number of immigrants
Mexico	143,446
China	80,167
India	69,013
Philippines	57,011
Dominican Republic	46,109
Cuba	36,452
Vietnam	34,157
South Korea	22,824
Colombia	22,635
Haiti	22,111
Iraq	21,133
Jamaica	19,662
El Salvador	18,667
Bangladesh	16,707
Pakistan	15,556

Source: 2011 Yearbook of Immigration Statistics

high-tech the most
advanced technology
available

60   One recent study found that more than half of the new technology companies in Silicon Valley were started by immigrants. Supporters also point out that new immigrants contribute to society just as the immigrant grandparents of many Americans did: They increase the nation's productivity by buying homes, starting new businesses, 65 and paying taxes, and they add to the diversity and excitement of American culture.

English is the dominant language in the United States, but 55 million people speak a language other than English in their home. Spanish is the second-most widely spoken language, with 34.6 million speakers in 2007. However, many other languages are spoken. Some have more speakers today than 30 years ago; others have fewer speakers.

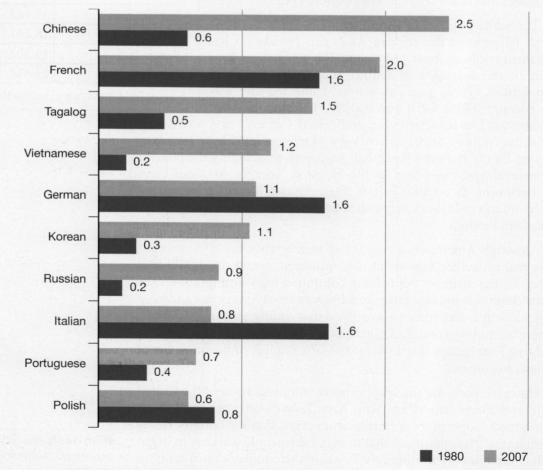

Languages other than English and Spanish spoken in U.S. homes in 1980 and 2007 (in millions)

Language	1980	2007
Chinese	0.6	2.5
French	1.6	2.0
Tagalog	0.5	1.5
Vietnamese	0.2	1.2
German	1.6	1.1
Korean	0.3	1.1
Russian	0.2	0.9
Italian	1..6	0.8
Portuguese	0.4	0.7
Polish	0.8	0.6

■ 1980   ■ 2007

Sources: **Modern Language Association, U.S. Census Bureau**

1 Answering true/false questions Ⓐ

One common question type on tests is the true/false question. Here are some strategies for answering this type of question.

- Most tests with true/false questions have an approximately equal number of true statements and false statements.
- Be careful of statements with negatives in them. These can be confusing. Remember that a negative statement that is correct is true.
- Be careful of statements containing words like *never*, *always*, *only*, and *all*. These are often false.
- Statements containing words such as *often*, *many*, and *sometimes* are often true.

A Read the statements below. Write *T* (true) or *F* (false). Base your answers on the text, the boxed text, and/or Figure 4.1.

_____ **1.** One of the factors in the nation's increasing diversity is the change in immigration policy.

_____ **2.** Immigration rates are the only factor in recent population growth.

_____ **3.** Whites are not the majority in the country anymore.

_____ **4.** A significant number of immigrants still come from Europe.

_____ **5.** Many technology companies were started by immigrants.

_____ **6.** Fifty-five million people in the country speak Spanish in their home.

B Next to your answer for each statement in Step A, write where you found the information: *Figure 4.1*, *Text*, or *Boxed Text*.

2 Writing descriptions Ⓦ

Adjective clauses describe nouns or noun phrases and begin with *that*, *which*, and *who*. Adjective clauses can be reduced to phrases that begin with an *-ing* form. In academic texts, these phrases are often used in descriptions, so you should become familiar with them.

	noun	adjective clause

There has been an increase in the number of *people* **who live in large cities**.

	noun	*-ing* phrase

There has been an increase in the number of *people* **living in large cities**.

	noun	adjective clause

The students read about a *study* **that showed an increase in immigrant businesses**.

	noun	*-ing* phrase

The students read about a *study* **showing an increase in immigrant businesses**.

A Read the sentences. Underline the adjective phrase that describes the noun or noun phrase in **bold**. Then rewrite each phrase as a full adjective clause. The first one is done as an example.

1. School districts in big cities report that they serve **immigrant children** from all over the world <u>speaking more than a hundred different languages</u>.

   <u>who speak more than a hundred different languages</u>

2. Approximately 12 percent of **the people** living in the United States were born in another country. _____

3. Many citizens protested against a **report** criticizing new immigrants.

   _____

4. They point out that many of **the people** working in high-tech companies are immigrants. _____

B Underline the *-ing* adjective phrase in the sentences. Then complete the sentences with your own advice.

1. Students taking important exams should _____

   _____ .

2. People learning a second language should _____

   _____ .

3. Tourists visiting (fill in a country or city of your choice) should _____

   _____ .

4. People earning more than $1 million a year should _____

   _____ .

3 Suffixes Ⓥ

> Suffixes are word endings that usually change a word from one part of speech to another but keep the basic meaning the same. One common suffix, *-(i)ty*, changes an adjective to a noun. Sometimes the spelling or pronunciation of the word changes when a suffix is added.
>
> *possible* ➜ *possibility*
> *necessary* ➜ *necessity*

A Look at the adjectives in the list below. The noun forms of <u>five</u> of these words are in the text. Find the noun forms in the text and mark them. Look up unfamiliar words in the dictionary.

| certain | real | productive | diverse | active | legal |
| ethnic | major | hostile | equal | popular | minor |

B Complete the sentences with words from Step A. Use the correct noun or adjective form.

1. The 2010 census makes it clear that the _____ of the U.S. population is increasing.

2. The Fourteenth Amendment guarantees that all people living in the United States receive _____ treatment.

3. Surveys have shown that a _____ of the United States population feels positive about immigration.

4. The largest number of _____ immigrants in the United States comes from Asia.

5. Critics who oppose high immigration rates must face _____ . If there are better jobs in the United States than in other countries, immigration will continue.

C Choose two words from Step A and write a sentence for each with the adjective in the noun form (*-ity*).

4 Thinking about the topic ®

Discuss the following questions with a partner or small group.

1. In the early twentieth century, Americans usually described their country as a *melting pot*. Today, Americans often describe their country as a *salad bowl* or a *mosaic*. What do these terms mean? Why do you think Americans today do not use the term *melting pot*? Look the words up in a dictionary if you need to.

Salad bowl

Melting pot

Mosaic

2. Is increasing diversity in the United States positive, negative, or both? Explain.

3. Will the trend toward increasing diversity in the United States continue? What could stop it?

Examining graphics ⓡ

A This reading is about the two fastest-growing minorities in the United States: Latinos and Asian Americans. The terms *Latinos* and *Hispanics* describe people who have come from, or whose family has come from, Spanish-speaking countries. The maps below show the percentage change in these two populations in the decade between 2000 and 2010. Work with a partner and study the maps.

Asian Americans % change 2000–2010

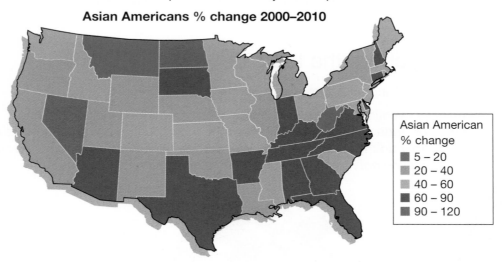

Asian American
% change
■ 5 – 20
■ 20 – 40
■ 40 – 60
■ 60 – 90
■ 90 – 120

Latinos % change 2000–2010

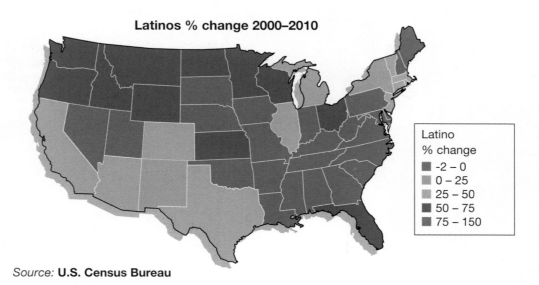

Latino
% change
■ -2 – 0
■ 0 – 25
■ 25 – 50
■ 50 – 75
■ 75 – 150

Source: **U.S. Census Bureau**

B Discuss these questions.

1. In what part of the country is the Asian American population growing fastest?
2. In what part of the country is the Latino population growing fastest?
3. Is percentage change related to the actual size of the two populations?

Reading 2

THE NATION'S FASTEST-GROWING MINORITIES

Two important minority groups have shown significant and continuous growth in recent years: Latinos and Asian Americans. Latinos have passed African Americans as the nation's largest minority group. However, since 2008, the largest number of legal immigrants has come
5 from Asia. The Asian American population grew faster than any other group during the period 2000–2010.

Latinos – The nation's largest minority

Figures from the 2000 census showed that Latinos (Hispanics) had become the nation's largest minority group. In the next 10 years, the population continued to expand – by 43 percent. This growth
10 rate of the Latino population was more than four times higher than the growth rate of the total population. The increase in the Latino population accounted for half of the growth in the total U.S. population between 2000 and 2010. This figure is the combined result of immigration and a birthrate that is considerably higher than the
15 rate in the general population.

At more than 50 million, Latinos are now 16 percent of the population. Cities with large Latino populations have traditionally been in big cities such as Miami, Los Angeles, and Houston, but now at least 28 cities across the country have Latino populations of more
20 than 100,000. Latinos have also moved to states without such big cities. In South Carolina and Alabama, for example, the Latino population tripled between 2000 and 2010. Experts predict that by 2050, the number of Latinos will be more than 100 million, almost a quarter of the U.S. population (see Figure 4.2).

Figure 4.2 Predicted growth in Latino and Asian-American populations

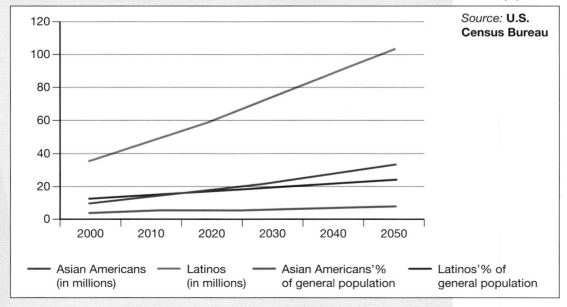

Source: **U.S. Census Bureau**

Asian Americans (in millions)	Latinos (in millions)	Asian Americans'% of general population	Latinos'% of general population

25 In 1965, Asian Americans were barely 1 percent of the population. Today, the number is about 5 percent and is growing rapidly, mostly as a result of immigration. In the past, Asians took jobs with low pay and were the targets of discrimination. Like other immigrants to the United States, they came because of poor economic conditions in their

30 countries. In the twenty-first century, this is no longer the case. China, India, and South Korea are prosperous, with healthy economies. There are many opportunities in those countries for ambitious people with skills and education.

However, Asians continue to immigrate to the United States

35 today because they still believe it will provide more opportunities for them. In contrast to Asian immigrants a century ago, many of today's Asian immigrants are highly educated and often work in the high-tech sector. More than 60 percent of adult Asian immigrants arrive in the United States with a college degree. They also have the

40 highest **median household income** of any group, including whites (see Figure 4.3).

median household income the middle amount of income of all people 15 years old or older in a household

Figure 4.3 Median household income 2010

Source: **U.S. Census Bureau**

Intermarriage in the Asian American community

Asian Americans are also more likely than any other minority group to marry outside of their community. Twenty-nine percent of Asian Americans who married between 2008 and 2010 married a non-Asian. The number was higher for women (37%) than for men (17%). Japanese Americans are the most likely to marry outside of their group (55%), and Indian Americans are the least likely (12%). The most famous recent Asian American bride is Dr. Priscilla Chan, who married Mark Zuckerberg, founder of Facebook, in 2012.

1 Reading for main ideas ®

A Each sentence below expresses a main idea in the reading. Match each sentence to a paragraph. Write the correct paragraph number in the blank.

_____ **a.** Latinos no longer live only in big cities.

_____ **b.** Asian immigrants today are very different from the Asian immigrants of the past.

_____ **c.** Latinos are the largest minority in the nation.

_____ **d.** The Asian American and Latino populations are growing faster than the white and black populations.

_____ **e.** Asians continue to immigrate to the United States for job opportunities.

B Put the main ideas in the correct order. Write them on a separate piece of paper.

2 Taking notes in an outline Ⓐ

> Using an outline can be an effective way to take notes. Numbers and letters are used to show relationships between ideas in the text. Making an outline of a text is a good way to prepare for tests and writing assignments.

Make an outline like the one below. Fill in the main ideas from the previous task and add supporting details. Add lines (*C*, *D*, etc.) to add more details. You may also use information from the graphs as support. Use your own words. The first main idea is done as an example. You do not need to write complete sentences for the details.

The nation's fastest-growing minorities

I. _The Asian American and Latino populations are growing faster than the white and black populations._ (Par. 1 main idea)

  A. _____ (Par. 1 detail)

  B. _____ (Fig. 4.2 detail)

II. _____ (Par. 2 main idea)

  A. _____ (Par. 2 detail)

  B. _____ (Par. 2 detail)

III. _____ (Par. 3 main idea)

  A. _____ (Par. 3 detail)

  B. _____ (Par. 3 detail)

IV. _____ Par. 4 main idea)

  A. _____ (Par. 4 detail)

  B. _____ (Par. 4 detail)

V. _____ (Par. 5 main idea)

  A. _____ (Par. 5 detail)

  B. _____ (Par. 5 detail)

3 Examining graphics ⓡ

A Review the maps on page 84 and Figure 4.2. Match the information below with its source. Write *M* for map and *F* for Figure 4.2.

_____ **1.** The percentage of Latinos in the population in 2010

_____ **2.** The percentage change in the Latino population between 2000 and 2010

_____ **3.** The number of Asian Americans in the nation in 2010

_____ **4.** The change in the Asian American population between 2000 and 2010

_____ **5.** The predicted Latino population in 2020

_____ **6.** The percentage of Asian Americans in the nation in 2000

_____ **7.** The percentage change in the Asian American population between 2000 and 2010

B Look at the chart below. It shows the number of Latinos who could have voted in the past four presidential elections and the number who actually voted. Based on the information in this chart and in Figure 4.2, discuss the following questions with a partner or a small group.

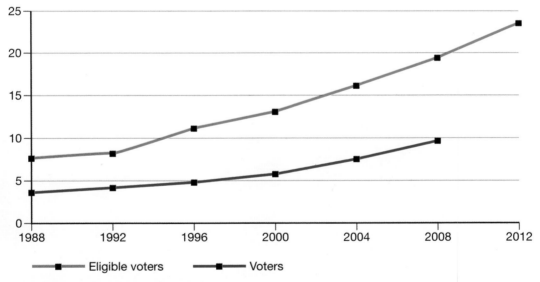

Latino participation in presidential elections, 1988-2012 (*in millions*)

Source: **Pew Research Hispanic Center**

1. How could an increasing Latino population affect the nation in 25 years? In 50 years?

2. How could a growing Asian American population affect the nation?

3. In what ways are these effects similar?

4. In what ways are they different?

4 Writing about growth Ⓦ

In academic writing, you will see certain phrases that describe change and growth. These phrases are made from combinations of certain words. Some are shown in the chart below. For example:

significant increase   expanding rapidly

A Study the chart. The words in each row can be combined in different ways to form a phrase about change or growth. The adjectives can modify either noun. The verbs and adverbs can be mixed. Find examples of these words and phrases in the text. Underline them.

	Adjective	Noun	Verb	Adverb
Row 1	considerable continuous significant steady	growth increase		
Row 2			grow expand increase rise	fast (er/est) quickly* rapidly* by _____ percent

* Adverbs that can go before or after the verb.

B Write three sentences about Figure 4.2 or the maps on page 84. Use appropriate combinations of words from the chart.

1 Words related to the topic Ⓥ

Academic texts often contain specialized vocabulary. Sometimes these words may be new to you. In other cases, they may be familiar words with a somewhat different meaning. This text contains some specialized legal vocabulary, that is, words related to the law.

A The text "The Undocumented: Unauthorized Immigrants" describes people who live in a country illegally. Study the definitions and the chart that follows.

Vocabulary related to law

undocumented: without official or legal papers that allow someone to work or live somewhere

unauthorized: without official permission to do something or be in a particular place

deport: to force someone to leave a country, especially someone who has no legal right to be there

Illegal	Legal
undocumented resident	legal resident
unauthorized immigrant	legal immigrant

B Look at Figure 4.4. Use the information to write a sentence about the following:

- undocumented residents
- unauthorized immigrants

2 Thinking about the topic Ⓡ

Discuss the following questions with a partner.

1. Why do people become unauthorized immigrants?

2. What do you think their lives are like?

Reading 3

THE UNDOCUMENTED: UNAUTHORIZED IMMIGRANTS

visa a document that lets you enter or leave a country

In order to come live and work in the United States, noncitizens need a special **visa**. It is difficult to get this kind of visa. Usually they are only given to people with special skills or those with family already in the country. Even these people must wait a long time for permission to come to the United States. For those who have little hope of getting this kind of visa, entering the country illegally may seem like the only choice. In 2010, about 11 million unauthorized, or illegal, immigrants – also sometimes called *undocumented residents* – were living in the United States. Most unauthorized immigrants come from Mexico; most others come from other parts of Latin America and from Asia (see Figure 4.4).

Most unauthorized immigrants enter the United States through the desert across the U.S.–Mexico border. These numbers have declined in recent years for several reasons. First, the economy of Mexico has improved since 2000, when about 500,000 people crossed the border illegally every year in search of work. In addition, the U.S. economy has been weak, so there are fewer jobs. As a result, the number of Mexicans crossing the border illegally is now estimated to be about 150,000 per year. Experts believe more people are returning to Mexico from the United States than are coming from Mexico to the United States.

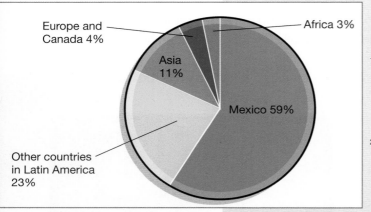

Figure 4.4 The undocumented population of the United States

Source: **Pew Research Hispanic Center**

minimum wage the lowest hourly rate of pay allowed by law

The main reason illegal immigrants come is for jobs. They are willing to do hard work that pays very little – on farms, in restaurants, and in factories. Many undocumented women care for children or the elderly; many undocumented men work as gardeners or in home repair and construction. For some illegal immigrants, even a job that pays below the **minimum wage** seems like a good opportunity. A recent study showed that many illegal immigrants had jobs in their home countries, but they could not support their families on their wages. They come to the United States for jobs that pay better so they can send money home to their families. It is estimated that 5.2 percent of the American workforce is undocumented.

Companies hire undocumented workers because they cost less than legal residents. Because they are undocumented, the workers usually do not complain if their pay is low, if they are treated badly, or if they are fired. Furthermore, the companies often do not give them benefits like health insurance. All of this helps to lower the cost of doing business and makes hiring undocumented workers seem like a good idea to many business owners.

After they arrive in the United States, undocumented
immigrants live with the fear that the police will catch them and
deport them. They try to avoid the police and other authorities. If
they find work, they often stay and start families. The Fourteenth
Amendment specifies that anyone who is born in the United
States is a citizen even if the parents are not legal residents. This
sometimes leads to divided families: Some family members
are citizens, but others may be deported if they are caught.

Undocumented residents who come at a very young age face
special problems. They do not remember their "home" country or
culture; some of them speak only English. The United States is the
only home that they know, yet, they are living in the country illegally.
Some lawmakers are trying to find a way to help them. They proposed
the Dream Act, which states that undocumented residents who
immigrated as children can remain if they go to college or serve in the
military. Congress debated the Dream Act in 2010 but did not pass it.
Supporters hope to try again.

Some Americans oppose these ideas and support the deportation
of all unauthorized immigrants. They would like to see better control
of the nation's borders. Others believe that these immigrants make
an important economic contribution to the country. Although the
subject of unauthorized immigration is controversial, most people
agree that as long as there are more jobs and better opportunities in
the United States than in immigrants' home countries, immigrants
will try to enter the country illegally.

Crossing the border can be dangerous. The United States watches many of the crossing points and stops any unauthorized immigrants who try to cross. As a result, many people have tried to cross from Mexico to the United States through the desert at points where there are few U.S. officials. Some of them do not bring enough food or water. Some get lost. Other people hide in ships and trucks. In 2010, U.S. officials stopped about half a million people from illegally entering the country. They also found the bodies of more than 400 people who died on the journey.

1 Reading actively ®

To understand a reading well and to remember what you have read, you need to read actively. One way to read actively is to look for and respond to the cues in the text. Find the cues and ask yourself questions. Cues can indicate the relationship of ideas and help you predict what will come next.

A Study the cues. Look at the questions to ask yourself.

Cues	Actions
. . . for several reasons. There are several factors . . .	What are the reasons, factors? Scan ahead and look for sequencing words such as *first, second* and so forth, to help you find reasons or factors.
(The) First . . .	What is (the) next? Look for a sequence. There must be at least one more. Look for the second and possibly a third one.
In addition, furthermore, also . . .	What came before? In addition to what? Go back and look. A discussion point is being added.
However . . .	What things is the writer contrasting? Contrasts show differences, as in X vs. Y. Go back and find the X that will be compared to the Y.
As a result . . .	This indicates a cause-effect relationship. What was the cause? Go back and find the cause.
Some . . .	Are there others? Is this a contrast? Look ahead to find out.

B Reread this excerpt from the text. Find the cues and underline them. Then follow the instructions for "Actions" in the chart.

> Most unauthorized immigrants enter the United States through the desert across the U.S.–Mexico border. These numbers have declined in recent years for several reasons. First, the economy of Mexico has improved since 2000, when about 500,000 people crossed the border illegally every year in search of work. In addition, the U.S. economy has been weak, so there are fewer jobs. As a result, the number of Mexicans crossing the border illegally is now estimated to be about 150,000 per year. Experts believe more people are returning to Mexico from the United States than are coming from Mexico to the United States.

C Explain to a partner what you did in response to each cue. Discuss how the cues show the relationship of ideas in the paragraph.

D Reread the boxed text and follow the same steps.

2 Using a dictionary Ⓥ

> Sometimes you cannot figure out a word's meaning from its context, and you will have to look it up in a dictionary. Some words have more than one meaning. It is important to choose the right meaning for the context.

A Read the different meanings of these words in the text.

support
1. (verb) to provide someone with money or other things that they need
   He supported his children until they went to college.
2. (verb) to give approval for
   The senator supports the president's plan.
3. (verb) to show that something is true
   The examples support her argument.

treat
1. (verb) to act in a particular way toward someone
   He does not treat his workers very well.
2. (verb) to give medical care
   The doctors are treating her for cancer.
3. (verb) to pay for someone else
   She treated her friends to a pizza.

B Find these words in the text and write the number of the correct meaning in Step A in the blank.

_____ support (Line 33)

_____ treat (Line 39)

_____ support (Line 61)

C With a partner, discuss whether any of the words in the context helped you choose the correct meaning.

D Remember to write new words and their definitions in your vocabulary notebook.

3 Thinking about the topic Ⓡ

Work with a partner or a small group. Think of some other countries with a lot of immigrants and discuss the following questions.

1. Where do most of the immigrants come from?
2. Why did they immigrate?
3. What challenges do they face in their new country(ies)?

4 Understanding cartoons ®

Cartoons use humor and pictures to make a point. They can often express ideas more quickly than words.

Work with a partner or a small group to complete the following activities.

A Look again at the cartoon from page 93. Identify the three groups that are represented.

B Answer these questions about the cartoon.

1. Who does the group on the left – a man, a woman, and a child – represent?
   _____
2. Who does the figure on the right represent? _____
3. Who does the man in the middle represent? _____

C Discuss these questions.

1. What is the message of the cartoon?
2. Is the cartoon amusing? Did it make you smile? Why or why not?
3. How would the groups that are represented feel about the cartoon? Why?

Chapter 4 Academic Vocabulary Review

The following words appear in the readings in Chapter 4. They all come from the Academic Word List, a list of words that researchers have discovered occur frequently in many different types of academic texts. For a complete list of all the Academic Word List words in this chapter and in all the readings in this book, see the Appendix on page 206.

approximately	decline (v)	furthermore	predict
authorities	dominant	income	stable
debated	founders	minimum	targets

Complete the sentences with words from the lists.

1. Experts _____ that Latinos will be almost one-quarter of the population in 2050.
2. One of the _____ of Google was born in Russia and came to the U.S. when he was six.
3. The average annual _____ of Asian Americans is $66,000.
4. English is _____ in the United States, but Spanish is also an important language.
5. Experts say that _____ 150,000 people crossed the Mexican border illegally into the United States in 2011.
6. The two speakers _____ the new government policy; one opposed the policy, and the other supported it.
7. The number of undocumented residents living in the country has remained _____ in the last few years.
8. Immigrants and minorities are sometimes the _____ of hostility and violence.
9. In 2007, the _____ wage in the United States rose to $7.25 per hour.
10. The number of unauthorized immigrants entering the country _____ between 2000 and 2012.

Practicing
Academic Writing

In this unit, you have read about the history of immigration in the United States. You will do a writing assignment based on what you have learned. In this assignment, you will use the pre-writing skills you practiced in Developing Writing Skills in Chapter 3.

American ambivalence: Immigration and diversity

Many Americans are ambivalent about immigration and the diversity it brings to the country. Your assignment is to write two paragraphs that describe these contrasting feelings.

PREPARING TO WRITE

A Look up *ambivalent/ambivalence* in an English dictionary. Consider the summary of attitudes in the last part of Reading 1 in Chapter 4. In a small group, discuss how the term *ambivalence* applies to attitudes to legal immigration and diversity in the United States.

B With your group, discuss what you have read in this unit. Take notes.

- What are the key points of this issue for Americans? (types and skills of immigrants, numbers and quotas, general influence in culture, etc.)
- What positive attitudes do Americans have toward immigration?
- What negative attitudes do Americans have?
- Have these changed over time? How? Why?

C Return to the texts in the unit and use the strategy you learned in Developing Writing Skills in Chapter 3. Make a chart like the one below and fill in examples, facts, and any other information about American attitudes and actions.

Positive attitudes and actions		Negative attitudes and actions	
In the past	Today	In the past	Today
New start for immigrants	Exciting mix of cultures	immigrants are too different	Immigrants take away jobs

D Review the information in your chart. You need to choose which information from your charts to use in your writing assignment. Which facts/examples do you think are the strongest evidence for positive attitudes? Which present the strongest evidence of negative attitudes? Choose two and highlight them.

Paragraph unity

When all information in one paragraph is related, this is called *paragraph unity*. A unified paragraph has a single focus, and each sentence connects to the focus and supports it.

E Practice identifying *unified* paragraphs in which all of the information is related. Read the three paragraphs below. Each makes two points about the difficult experiences of Chinese immigrants. They all begin with the same point about discrimination and hostility against these immigrants, specifically:

1. Discrimination and hostility about what? – *employment*
2. Discrimination and hostility when? – *in the nineteenth century*

All three paragraphs also include a second point, which is in **bold**. These second points are also about an aspect of the challenges faced by Chinese immigrants. For the **bold** sentences in each paragraph, try to answer the same questions:

1. Discrimination and hostility about what?
2. Discrimination and hostility when?

_____ **a.** In the nineteenth century, Chinese immigrants experienced difficulties in the United States. One problem that many immigrants faced was discrimination at work. They had to take the most difficult and low-paying jobs and in some cases, employers refused to hire them. **Today Chinese immigrants face hostility because many Americans just don't understand their culture. They think they are too different and will never become real Americans.**

_____ **b.** In the nineteenth century, Chinese immigrants experienced difficulties in the United States. One problem that many immigrants faced was discrimination at work. They had to take the most difficult and low-paying jobs and in some cases, employers refused to hire them. **Outside of the workplace, they also faced discrimination. Chinese immigrants were often mistreated by Americans and other immigrants. The Chinese seemed very different to them and they did not understand Chinese culture or customs. The result was hostility and sometimes violence.**

_____ **c.** In the nineteenth century, Chinese immigrants experienced difficulties in the United States. One problem that many immigrants faced was discrimination at work. They had to take the most difficult and low-paying jobs and in some cases, employers refused to hire them. **Today Chinese immigrants still face hostility in the workplace because many Americans believe they are taking jobs away from Americans. Some things have not changed much.**

F *Two* of the paragraphs are *unified*; that is, all of the information is related to one idea. The information in these paragraphs fits well together. One paragraph includes information about different ideas that do not fit well together. It is not unified. With your partner, decide which paragraphs have unity. Put a check (✓) in front of the unified paragraphs. Explain the reasons for your choices.

G Think about the two paragraphs that you checked in Step F. With a partner, decide what the topic of each unified paragraph is. Make sure the topics are broad enough to include all of the points in the paragraph. Write them on a separate sheet of paper.

H Write a topic sentence for each of the unified paragraphs. Remember that the topic sentence should state the topic and make a claim about it.

Notice that you were able to write a topic sentence about two unified paragraphs. It would be difficult to write a topic sentence for the paragraph that you did not check (✓) in Step F because it is not unified around a single focus.

I Now think about the ideas in your chart that you selected in Step D. Can you write unified paragraphs with the evidence that you highlighted? Is your positive evidence all positive? Is your negative evidence all negative? Check with your partner. Go back to your chart and make new choices if necessary.

NOW WRITE

A Review the Practicing Writing Skills sections about topic sentences and expressing ideas in your own words. Write a topic sentence for each of your paragraphs.

B Review the chart in Step C above and the two pieces of information you have found that will support each topic sentence. Write your two paragraphs as in the diagram below.

- Be sure to put the text away before you begin writing so you can write in your own words.
- Be sure your paragraphs are unified, that all sentences are related to one topic.

Paragraph 1	Topic sentence about positive aspects + Two supporting details
Paragraph 2	Topic sentence about negative aspects + Two supporting details

C You now have two separate, unified paragraphs. You need to write a little bit more so you can introduce the topic to your reader. Think about the discussion you had with your classmates about ambivalence at the beginning of this activity. Ambivalence is an idea that can connect your two paragraphs. Write a sentence about ambivalence toward immigration and diversity. Use the word bank below to help you.

immigration/ immigrants	attitude/ feeling	Americans	ambivalent/ ambivalence	diversity

This sentence will appear at the beginning of your piece of writing, as shown by the green box in the diagram in step B.

Transition Markers

Transition words and phrases signal the relationship between ideas in your writing and help readers understand how the text is organized. Transitions may mark a time sequence, cause and effect, contrast, additional information, or other relationships. There are different transitions to connect, nouns, phrases, clauses and sentences. Choosing the appropriate transition marker can help make your writing clearer.

D Your first paragraph is about positive attitudes. Your second paragraph is about negative attitudes. They represent opposite, or contrasting, perspectives. It is helpful to readers if you give them a signal when you make this kind of transition. In this case, you need a transition word or phrase that marks this contrast. Here are some contrast markers that you can use to begin your second paragraph:

> *On the other hand,* Americans also . . .
>
> *In contrast,* other Americans/sometimes Americans . . .
>
> *However,* not all Americans/sometimes Americans also . . .

Add a transition expression at the beginning of the second paragraph, as shown by the blue box in the diagram in step B. Now put all the pieces of your writing together.

AFTER YOU WRITE

A Reread your own paragraphs. Check that:

- the topic sentences make a clear claim
- your paragraphs have two examples
- you have used terms from the readings

B Exchange papers with a partner. Discuss the following questions about your paragraphs.

- Does the first sentence say what the piece of writing will be about?
- Does your partner have a good topic sentence for each paragraph?
- Does your partner have appropriate, clear examples of the positive side (Par. 1)?
- Does your partner have appropriate, clear examples of the negative side (Par. 2)?
- Is each paragraph unified?
- Is there a transition between the two topics?

C Revise your work. Use your partner's suggestions and your own ideas.

D Edit your paragraphs.

- Look for errors in spelling and grammar.
- Make corrections wherever you find errors.

Unit 3
The Struggle for Equality

In this unit, you will look at the idea of equality: how it was viewed in the early days of the nation, how various groups have struggled to achieve it, how it has changed, and how Americans view the concept today. In Chapter 5, you will focus on the historical foundations of the struggle for equality. In Chapter 6, you will examine the concept of equality in its current context, especially with regard to groups who are still fighting for equal access and opportunity. You will explore how government and society have tried to correct past discrimination and how well they have succeeded.

Contents

In Unit 3, you will read and write about the following topics.

Skills

In Unit 3, you will practice the following skills.

R Reading Skills	**W Writing Skills**
Increasing reading speed Thinking about the topic Predicting Reading for details Reading boxed texts Understanding key terms Reading for main ideas Pronoun reference Applying what you have read Examining graphics Reading about statistics	Writing about time sequences Understanding text structure Markers of relationship Writing about examples Writing about obligations and recommendations Writing about statistics
V Vocabulary Skills	**A Academic Success Skills**
Suffixes Words related to the topic Guessing meaning from context Synonyms Prepositions with verbs	Answering definition questions on a test Answering short-answer test questions Reviewing for a test

Learning Outcomes

Write two paragraphs presenting a point of view on equal rights and equal protection

Previewing the Unit

Before reading a unit (or chapter) in a textbook, it is a good idea to preview the contents page and think about the topics that will be covered. This will help you understand how the unit is organized and what it is going to be about.

Read the contents page for Unit 3 on page 104 and do the following activities.

Chapter 5: The Struggle Begins

In the first chapter of this unit, you are going to read about historical ideas of equality in the United States. You will also examine some of the effects of these ideas on society.

A Look at the photograph and answer these questions with a partner.

1. What does the sign mean?

2. When and where was the photograph taken?

B Discuss these questions with your partner or in a small group.

1. Is the young man doing something "wrong"?

2. What do you think he is thinking?

Chapter 6: The Struggle Continues

In the second chapter of this unit, you are going to read about modern ideas of equality. You will also look at the continuing and new issues in the struggle for equality.

A Take this survey about equality and success. Check (✓) how much you agree or disagree with each statement. Use your knowledge of the United States or another country you know well to answer. 1 = Strongly agree 5 = Strongly disagree

Statements about equality	1	2	3	4	5
1. Everyone is equal at birth.					✓
2. Everyone has an equal chance of success.					✓
3. Everyone is treated equally by the government.					✓
4. Everyone is treated equally in the educational system.					✓
5. Everyone is treated equally at work.					✓
6. Success depends on your achievement.	✓				
7. Success depends on who you are and who you know.					✓

B Compare your survey results in a small group. Discuss the similarities and differences. What are some of the reasons for the similarities and differences?

Chapter 5
The Struggle Begins

1 Increasing reading speed ⓡ

A Review the strategies for increasing your reading speed on page 77.

B Read "All Men Are Created Equal," using these strategies.

  1. Before you begin, enter your starting time: _11:05_
  2. After you finish, enter your ending time: _11:08_

C Calculate your reading speed:

Number of words in the text (540) ÷

Number of minutes it took you to read the text = your Reading Speed

Reading speed: _2m 53 sec_

Your goal should be about 150–180 words per minute.

D Check your reading comprehension   ext.

  1. What is the main idea of the read
  2. What ideas in the Declaration of I
  3. How did the meaning of equality
  4. What was the purpose of the Fou

Handwritten note:
1- Equality between black and white people.
2- Inequality society.
3 -
4. Equal protection of the law to everyone in the USA.

2 Thinking about the top

The Declaration of Independence wa
in 1776. The title of the text you are
Declaration: ". . . all men are created

A Think about these questions.

  • What did the authors mean by "al

  • What does the term *equality* mean to you?

  • Can the meaning of *equality* change?

B Discuss your ideas with a partner.

Reading 1

ALL MEN ARE CREATED EQUAL

The meaning of equality to the founders of the United States

The idea of equality was essential to the founders of the United States, and it remains important in how Americans view themselves and their nation today. But what did the term *equality* really mean when the nation began? The most famous lines in the Declaration of
5 Independence, written in 1776, are:

> We hold these Truths to be self-evident, that all Men are created equal, that they are endowed by their Creator with certain unalienable Rights, that among these are Life, Liberty, and the Pursuit of Happiness.

In simpler, more modern language this means:

10 > It is clear that all men are equal at birth. God gives them certain rights that no one can take away: the right to live, the right to be free, and the right to try to have a life that will make them happy.

These ideas might seem simple and obvious today, but they were revolutionary in 1776, when many people accepted the idea
15 of inequality in society: Some people were born rich and powerful; others were born poor, and there was not much that people could do to change their place in society.

Thomas Jefferson wrote the Declaration of Independence. He and the other founders of the United States rejected the view that a person's
20 place in society is fixed. They brought together ideas from different sources, including English and French philosophers and American Indian tribes that had democratic systems of government. In 1789, the Constitution made the democratic idea of "one man–one vote" the law of the land. However, this view of equality did not include everyone.
25 When the Declaration of Independence and the Constitution were written, "men" did not mean "people." It excluded women, enslaved Africans, and American Indians.

The meaning of equality after the U.S. Civil War

Almost 100 years after the Declaration of Independence, the United States fought a **civil war** that involved the issue of equality. Although
30 most people in the North probably did not believe that white and black people were truly equal, many of them rejected the idea of slavery. In contrast, most Southerners supported slavery. This was partly because the economy of the Southern states depended on slaves. The disagreements between the North and the South finally resulted in a
35 civil war, which ended in 1865 with victory for the North.

During the Civil War, at a service to dedicate a cemetery for soldiers, President Abraham Lincoln made one of the most famous speeches in American history, the Gettysburg Address. In it, he reminded the American people of the famous words, "all men are
40 created equal." He stated that, "this nation, under God, shall have a new birth of freedom" and asked if the country was ready to keep the promise of the words in the Declaration of Independence.

Could the country accept the idea that all men are created equal – not just white men? The country struggled to answer Lincoln's
45 question. The Fourteenth Amendment to the Constitution was passed several years after the Civil War ended. It guarantees equal protection of the law to everyone in the United States. Yet, long after the Civil War, many Americans still did not receive equal treatment at work, at school, or in the courts.

civil war a war between two groups of people living in the same country

President Lincoln at Gettysburg

1 Thinking about the topic Ⓡ

A Read this passage about Thomas Jefferson's ideas.

Thomas Jefferson was the third president of the United States. Before he became president, he wrote the Declaration of Independence. He based some parts of the Declaration on the idea of *natural rights*, that is, rights that we have because we are human beings. In the Declaration of Independence, he uses the term *unalienable rights*, which means that no one can take these rights away – not a king and not the government. These rights include the right to live and to be free. Jefferson believed the government's most important purpose is to protect these natural rights. These ideas appear in the Declaration of Independence.

B Discuss these questions with a partner.

   1. How are Jefferson's ideas connected to the phrase "all men are created equal"?

   2. How were these ideas about the purpose of government different from earlier ideas?

2 Writing about time sequences Ⓦ

Time markers show when an event took place. Time markers signal a connection between two clauses or between a clause and a noun phrase.

Time markers between clauses		**Time markers between a clause and a noun phrase**	
after	until	after	during
before	while, when	before	until

Notice that *until*, *before*, and *after* are in both categories, but *while* and *when* can only connect clauses, and *during* can only connect a clause and a noun phrase. Here are some examples. Note the location of the marker.

clause 1	time marker*	clause 2
Cotton was the South's most important crop	**before**	the Civil War began.
Slaves carried their babies on their backs	**while**	they worked in the fields.

clause	time marker	noun phrase
Cotton was the South's most important crop	**before**	the Civil War.
African American men could not vote	**until**	the year 1870.

*The time marker begins the phrase or clause.

A Go back to the reading. Find a time marker between two clauses, and a time marker that connects a clause with a noun phrase.

B Read the sentences and circle the correct choice. If both are correct, circle both. Pay attention to the meaning of the time markers.

1. (*After the Civil War* / *After the Civil War ended*), Congress passed the Thirteenth, Fourteenth, and Fifteenth Amendments.
2. (*While* / *During*) the second half of the twentieth century, there was an increase in immigration from Latin America.
3. (*Before the War of Independence* / *Before the War of Independence began*), many colonists were British subjects.

C Write four sentences about your own life. Use each of these time markers: *before*, *after*, *until*, *while*, and *during*.

3 Suffixes ⓥ

Many verbs can be changed to nouns by adding a *suffix*, a word part that is added at the end of a word. Three common noun endings are *ance/ence*, *ment*, and *(i/a)tion/sion*. Note that small spelling changes sometimes occur.

Verb	Noun *ance/ence*	Noun *ment*	Noun *(i/a)tion/sion*
amend		amend*ment*	
appear	appear*ance*		
depend	depend*ence*		
define			defin*ition*
declare			declar*ation*
establish		establish*ment*	
govern		govern*ment*	

Look at the chart. Complete the sentences. Find a verb form in the text related to the nouns below. Find a noun form in the text related to the verbs below.

Nouns			Verbs
acceptance *accept*	involvement *involve*	disagree*ment*	
inclusion *include*	rejection *reject*	protect*ion*	
exclusion *exclude*	dedication *dedicate*	treat*ment*	

1. The *exclusion* of Native Americans, African Americans, and women from the early documents of the nation was accepted as normal in the eighteenth century.
2. The Fourteenth Amendment guarantees equal *protection* of all people.
3. The British king *rejected* the colonists' demand for greater participation in government.
4. Lincoln gave the Gettysburg Address at a *dedication* ceremony for soldiers who died in the war.
5. There is greater *acceptance* of diversity in the United States today than during the Civil War.

1 Words related to the topic Ⓥ

Work in a small group to complete the following act

A Look these words up in a dictionary and review thei

- discriminate / discrimination
- disenfranchise / disenfranchisement
- segr
- sepa

[handwritten note:]
1 - Discrimination Segregation
2 - Separation - divide something
segregation - Official practice of keeping people apart.
3 - Racial, sexism, religious, origin, disabilities.
4 - Women.

B Look at the photographs and discuss these questio

1. Which word(s) from Step A describe the situation
2. What is the difference between *separation* and *se*
3. What are some forms of *discrimination* that you h
4. What groups in addition to African Americans have been *disenfranchised* in the history of the United States? (Review Chapter 3 to find the answer if necessary.)

[handwritten:] sexism, religious, origin.

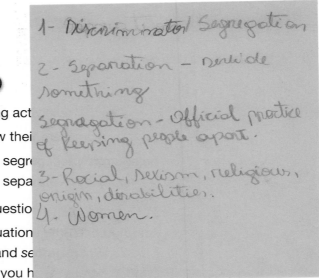

The words *colored* and *Negro* were used for African Americans until the 1960s. Today, we use the words *black* or *African American*.

2 Predicting Ⓡ

The title of the text you are going to read is "The Legacy of the Civil War." Look up *legacy* in your dictionary. Predict what the reading will be about with your group.

[handwritten:] – An amount of money or property left to someone in a will.

Reading 2

THE LEGACY OF THE CIVIL WAR

After the Civil War ended in 1865 with victory for the North, Congress passed the Thirteenth Amendment to the Constitution, freeing all slaves. The Fifteenth Amendment, which gave African American men the right to vote, followed in 1870. For a short time, the lives of
5 African Americans improved. However, the civil and political rights of African Americans were gradually taken away because states in the South began to pass laws that limited these rights. These new laws became known as *Jim Crow* laws. The Jim Crow laws created a system of disenfranchisement, segregation, and discrimination, primarily in
10 the South. Much of this system continued into the 1960s.

Jim Crow laws affected voting, the use of public facilities, and education. Starting in the 1880s, most Southern states passed laws requiring African Americans to pass *literacy tests* or pay a *voting tax* in order to vote. Literacy tests required voters to read a text and answer
15 questions about it. Often these texts were difficult and confusing. Because most African Americans had little or no education at that time, many of them failed the test. The voting tax required voters to pay to vote. The voting tax was one or two dollars, which was equal to several days' wages and far too expensive for many of the former
20 slaves. The test and the tax were effective ways to prevent African Americans from voting.

In addition, many Southern states passed *grandfather laws*, which stated that anyone with a family member (such as a grandfather) who had voted before 1867 did not have to take the literacy test or
25 pay voting taxes. This allowed uneducated, poor white voters to avoid these tests and taxes. Because the parents and grandparents of African Americans had been slaves and therefore unable to vote, the grandfather laws prevented many African Americans in the South from voting.

30 Racial inequality and discrimination were not limited to the South. A struggle for equality took place in other parts of the country. Many states had Jim Crow laws that required whites and African Americans to use separate public facilities, such as restaurants, hotels, waiting rooms in train stations, drinking fountains, and public toilets.
35 The white facilities were almost always superior to the facilities for African Americans. On trains and buses, African Americans had to sit in separate sections in the back. African Americans who tried to use white facilities could be arrested and sent to jail. There were also laws against interracial marriage in many states, both in the North and
40 South. Many of these laws remained in place until the 1960s.

Perhaps most important, in many places African Americans could not go to the same schools as whites. Instead, they went to separate schools for African Americans. These schools were usually not very good because they did not receive as much money from the government as white schools did. For many years, the courts supported these segregation laws. In a famous case in 1896, the Supreme Court ruled that segregation was legal if facilities were "separate but equal." In fact, facilities for whites and African Americans were almost never equal.

Finally, there were frequent threats against African Americans, even physical violence, to prevent them from voting and to maintain their low position in society. African Americans who tried to work against this system, even in small ways – for example, by arguing with a white person – might be beaten, or worse, *lynched*. A lynching is a murder that occurs, usually by hanging, when an angry individual or group decides that someone is guilty of a crime or misbehavior and kills the suspect without a trial. It is estimated that there were almost 5,000 lynchings between 1882 and 1968.

The struggle for equality was not over. From the beginning of the nation, through the Civil War, and still today, Americans have argued about what equality really means, and the fight for equality for all people has been long and difficult.

Madam C. J. Walker

In spite of the hardships, the period between the Civil War and the 1960s was a time of great cultural and artistic activity in the African American community. There was also an increase in the number of businesses operated by and for African Americans. Madam C. J. Walker ran one of the most successful businesses during this time.

Walker saw a business opportunity in her own community. There were not very many businesses that served African Americans. Her idea was to develop and sell hair-care products that were made specifically for African Americans. Starting in 1905, she went door to door to sell her products. Five years later, she had a factory that provided employment for some 3,000 people. By the time of her death in 1919, Walker was one of the first American women to become a millionaire.

Madam C. J. Walker

1 Reading for details Ⓡ

A Find and underline supporting evidence for these ideas in the text, including the boxed text. (Be careful; the items below do not follow the order of the text.)

1. There was physical violence against African Americans.
2. Southern leaders took several steps to disenfranchise African Americans.
3. Separate facilities for blacks and whites were not really equal.
4. Segregation did not prevent some African American businesses from succeeding.
5. The end of slavery did not bring equality for Southern blacks.

B Compare your answers in small groups.

2 Answering definition questions on a test Ⓐ

One common type of test question asks you to define important terms. Important words are often noted in a text in different ways.

- Boldfacing (**civil rights**)
- Italics (*civil rights*)

As you read, you should try to predict which definitions might be on a test. You can use the XYZ formula for writing definitions that you learned in Unit 1.

A Work with a partner. Review these key terms from the text. Take turns explaining what each term means in your own words.

1. Jim Crow laws
2. literacy tests
3. voting tax
4. grandfather laws
5. lynching

B Write a short definition for key terms in Readings 1 and 2. Do not look at the texts. (Review the XYZ formula for definitions on page 22 if necessary.)

1. **Literacy tests** were . . .
2. A **voting tax** was . . .
3. A **lynching** is . . .

C Write an expanded definition of Jim Crow laws. (Review expanded definitions in Writing Definitions on page 23.)

D Compare your expanded definition with a partner's.

E Go back to the text. Choose two terms that you think might be on a test. Did you write definitions for them in Step B? If not, then write them now.

3 Reading boxed texts ⓡ

Many academic textbooks include boxed texts. Boxed texts add interesting information that can deepen your understanding of the information in the main text. They can do the following:

- Give an interesting example of an idea in the main text
- Give some information, such as statistics, that is too detailed to include in the main text
- Give a definition
- Give some information or ideas that may be in conflict with the text
- Ghow how the ideas in the text apply to everyday life

A Reread the boxed text at the end of the reading.

B Which purpose applies to the boxed text?

C Discuss the information in the boxed text with a small group. How does it deepen your understanding of the main text?

4 Guessing meaning from context ⓥ

It is important to develop strategies for dealing with difficult or unfamiliar vocabulary, especially in academic textbooks. One key strategy is looking at the context – the words and sentences that come before and after the unknown word – for clues to a word's meaning. Clues may be:

- Examples
- Definitions
- Near-synonyms (words with almost the same meaning)
- Related ideas
- Parts of words

A Read the sentences from the text. Use the underlined context to figure out the meaning of the words in **bold**. Circle the letter of the correct definition.

1. The voting tax was <u>one or two dollars</u>. This was equal to several days' **wages** and was too expensive for many African Americans.

   a. cost   **b.** pay   **c.** journey

2. Many states had Jim Crow laws that required whites and African Americans to use separate **public facilities**, such as <u>restaurants, hotels, waiting rooms in train stations, drinking fountains, and public toilets</u>.

   a. buildings or services that people use

   b. equipment

   c. laws passed by the government

3. African Americans who tried to use white facilities could be **arrested** and <u>sent to jail</u>.

   a. hurt   **b.** punished   **c.** taken by the police

4. Finally, there were frequent threats against African Americans, even <u>physical violence</u>, to prevent them from voting and to maintain their low position in society. African Americans who tried to work against this system, even in small ways – for example, by arguing with a white person – might be **beaten**, <u>or worse</u>, *lynched*.

   a. hit very hard   **b.** killed   **c.** taken by the police

B Sometimes you can use more than one strategy to guess the meaning of an unfamiliar word. Read the sentence below. Use context clues and your knowledge of word parts to guess the meaning of the word in bold. Write a definition of the word in the blank.

There were also laws against **interracial** marriage in many states, both in the North and South.

   <u>Between races.</u>

C Compare your definition with a classmate's.

1 Thinking about the topic ®

A Read these excerpts of speeches by Dr. Martin Luther King Jr. He made the first one on August 28, 1963. More than 200,000 people joined him in demanding voting rights for African Americans and an end to segregation. The first is known as the "I have a dream" speech. The second excerpt is from his last speech five years later.

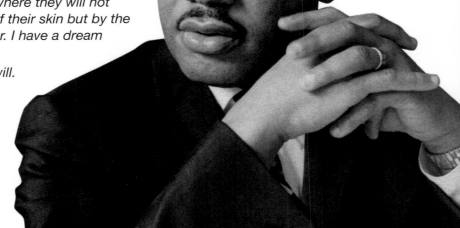

1. . . . *And so even though we face the difficulties of today and tomorrow, I still have a dream. . . . I have a dream my four little children will one day live in a nation where they will not be judged by the color of their skin but by the content of their character. I have a dream today!*

2. *I just want to do God's will. And He's allowed me to go up to the mountain. And I've looked over. And I've seen the Promised Land. I may not get there with you. But I want you to know tonight, that we, as a people, will get to the promised land!*

B Discuss these questions in a small group.

1. How would you describe King's dream?
2. What does "the content of their character" mean?
3. King used dramatic and colorful images, such as "up to the mountain." Why would he use the image of a mountain in this speech?
4. How are the ideas in these speeches related to what you have learned in this unit?

2 Understanding key terms ® Ⓥ

A Read the title of the text and then look at the definition below:

civil rights: the rights of each person in a society, including equality under the law and in employment and the right to vote

B Work in a small group. Compare *civil rights* to the *natural* (or *unalienable*) *rights* that Thomas Jefferson wrote about in the Declaration of Independence. (Review pages 107–108 if you do not remember).

Reading 3

THE BATTLE FOR CIVIL RIGHTS

During the 1950s and 1960s, African Americans continued their struggle for equality. They brought legal cases to court but also protested in the streets. Their efforts became known as the civil rights movement. The leaders of the movement wanted all forms of protest
5 to be peaceful and nonviolent.

In the courts

The U.S. Supreme Court had decided in 1896 that "separate but equal" facilities for blacks and whites were legal. By the 1950s, 21 states had segregated public schools. Most of the black schools were not as good as the white ones.

10   Oliver Brown of Topeka, Kansas, decided to challenge the 1896 Supreme Court decision. He asked the local school board to let his daughter attend a nearby white school. When the board refused, Brown sued them. The case of *Brown versus Board of Education of Topeka* eventually reached the Supreme Court (in 1953) and is one of
15 the most famous legal cases in U.S. history. The defenders of school segregation argued that states had a right to make decisions about social and educational issues and that segregation was not harmful to blacks. Lawyers for Brown argued that black and white schools were not equal and that the Fourteenth Amendment guarantees equal
20 treatment for everyone. The Supreme Court ruled in Brown's favor. The Chief Justice noted, "Separate educational facilities are inherently

unequal." In other words, the fact that the schools are separate means that they must be unequal. A year later, the Court ruled that laws permitting segregated schools were unconstitutional.

25   Many communities followed the court's order, but in other places, local and state governments refused. In 1957, the Arkansas governor tried to prevent African American students from attending the all-white high school in the state capital, Little Rock. President Dwight Eisenhower had to send in soldiers to protect them. Some communities
30 closed their public schools because they did not want black children to attend. Some white families took their children out of public schools and sent them to private schools. By 1960, in spite of the Supreme Court decision, less than 1 percent of black children in the South attended school with white children.

In the streets

35 Meanwhile, discrimination and segregation continued in many other areas of daily life, for example, in public transportation. In 1955, an African-American woman named Rosa Parks was riding a crowded bus in Montgomery, Alabama.
40 The driver ordered her to give her seat to a white man and move to the back of the bus. Parks refused, so the police arrested her. In response, African Americans in Montgomery decided to boycott the bus company, that is, not use the company's buses.
45 The boycott lasted for more than a year.

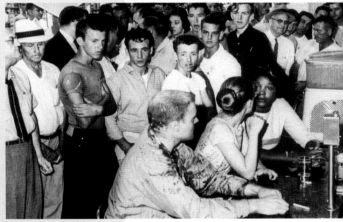

A sit-in at a lunch counter in Jackson, Mississippi, 1963

    Many college students, both black and white, joined the civil rights movement. In one famous incident at an all-white restaurant in North Carolina, black and white students organized a form of protest called a sit-in. They simply sat in the restaurant. They refused to leave until
50 the African American protesters were served. There were many sit-ins. Sometimes they lasted for days. Sometimes white customers in the restaurants shouted at the students, threw food at them, or hit them, but the students continued their protests. Sit-ins and other forms of protests spread across the South. Several cases were brought before
55 the Supreme Court. In the end, the Supreme Court ruled that the segregation on buses and in public facilities was illegal.

    In many places in the South, these protests angered white people. The anger sometimes led to violence against the protesters and even against blacks in general. Protests expanded, and the violence against them
60 also increased.

    In the mid-1960s, Congress passed two important laws. In 1964, the Civil Rights Act prohibited segregation in schools and public places and prohibited discrimination by employers.

In 1965, the Voting Rights Act gave the federal government the power
65 to make sure that African Americans were allowed to vote in elections.
Within a year, there were 230,000 new black voters. Thus began the
long process of gaining equality for African Americans, an effort that
continues today, in schools, in courts, and in the workplace.

Langston Hughes (1902–1967) was a poet and journalist who wrote about the lives of
ordinary African Americans. He is one of the greatest American poets of the twentieth
century. He wrote "Dream Deferred," below, in 1951. It is probably his most famous poem.

Dream Deferred
What happens to a dream deferred?
Does it dry up
like a raisin in the sun
Or fester like a sore –
And then run?
Does it stink like rotten meat?
Or crust and sugar over –
Like a syrupy sweet?

Maybe it just sags
like a heavy load.

Or does it explode?

1 Reading for main ideas ⓡ

Each paragraph has a main idea, but in short academic texts, there is also usually one central idea for the whole text. Two strategies that will help you identify the main idea of a whole text are:

- Reading the introductory paragraph of the text
- Reading the headings that organize the text

Reread the first paragraph and the headings of "The Battle for Civil Rights." Check (✓) the statement that expresses the main idea of the reading.

_____ **1.** The civil rights movement was a nonviolent form of protest that helped bring equal rights to black Americans.

_____ **2.** People fought in the courts and in the streets against Jim Crow laws.

_____ **3.** There were important court cases that helped encourage nonviolent protests against inequality.

___✓___ **4.** The civil rights movement used the legal system and nonviolent protest to bring equal rights to African Americans.

2 Pronoun reference ⓡ ⓦ

When you read academic texts, and when you do writing assignments, it is important to pay attention to pronouns, such as *he*, *she*, *it*, *they*, *his*, *her*, and *their*. These pronouns refer to people, things, or ideas that usually appeared in an earlier sentence.

Read these sentences from the text. Underline the people, things, or ideas that the pronouns in **bold** refer to. Draw an arrow between them.

1. In 1957, the Arkansas governor tried to prevent African American students from attending the all-white high school in the state capital, Little Rock. President Dwight Eisenhower had to send in soldiers to protect **them**.

2. Some communities closed **their** public schools because **they** did not want black children to attend. Some white families took **their** children out of public schools and sent **them** to private schools.

3. Sometimes white customers in the restaurants shouted at the students, threw food at **them**, or hit **them**, but the students continued **their** protests.

4. In one famous incident at an all-white restaurant in North Carolina, black and white students organized a protest called a sit-in. **They** simply sat in the restaurant until the African American protesters were served. There were many sit-ins. Sometimes **they** lasted for days.

5. The anger sometimes led to violence against the protesters and even against blacks in general. Protests expanded and the violence against **them** also increased.

3 Answering short-answer test questions Ⓐ

Personal informative speech

Short-answer tests usually include three types of questions. It is important to understand the language of the questions, and also to use the language when answering the questions. Use these two strategies:

1. Look at the verb in the question. What is the question asking you to do?
2. Use the language of the question to begin your answer. This will help you focus on the information you need to provide.

Look at these common verbs in test questions:

Verb	What the verb asks you to do
analyze	Divide something – for example, an idea, an event, or a series of events – into parts. Explain these parts. Say how they are related to each other.
describe	Discuss in detail the characteristics of an idea, event, etc.
compare / compare and contrast	Examine at least two ideas, events, etc. Say how they are similar or different.

A Read these examples of test questions based on this chapter.

1. **Analyze** the arguments for segregation in the *Brown versus Board of Education of Topeka* case.
2. **Describe** the strategies of the civil rights movement.
3. **Compare and contrast** the economies of the North and South before the U.S. Civil War.

B Write one new test question for each verb in Step A. Use content from any of the readings in this chapter.

C Read these examples of the beginnings of answers to the questions in Step A.

1. The lawyers defending segregation in the *Brown versus Board of Education of Topeka* case offered two main arguments.
2. The strategies of the civil rights movement included court battles and street protests.
3. The economies of the Northern and Southern states before the U.S. Civil War were very different.

D Notice that each statement in Step C contains two elements:

- The language of the original question
- Additional information that shows how the writer will answer the question

In each statement in Step C, underline the language from the question and circle the new information.

E Exchange the question you wrote in Step B with a partner. For your partner's question, write just the first sentence of your answer. Be sure to use the language of the question and include enough additional information to show how you would answer the question.

4 Reading boxed texts Ⓡ

Work in a small group to complete the following activities.

A Reread the poem in the boxed text on page 120. Discuss these questions.

1. Whose dream is Hughes writing about? MLK

2. What does Hughes mean by saying that the dream is "deferred"?
Look the term up in a dictionary and write the definition below.
Put off to a later time.

3. Hughes compares a deferred dream to five things. What are they? List them here.
Dried raisin
Sore
Run
Stink
Meat

4. Why does Hughes compare deferred dreams to the five things listed above?

5. What do *you* think happens to dreams that are deferred for too long? What would you compare your deferred dreams to?

B Compare "Dream Deferred" to Martin Luther King Jr.'s speech excerpts on page 120.

1. How do you think Hughes's "Dream Deferred" is related to King's dream?

2. Do Hughes and King have the same view about dreams?

3. How are these dreams connected to the struggle for equality?

Chapter 5 Academic Vocabulary Review

The following words appear in the readings in Chapter 5. They all come from the Academic Word List, a list of words that researchers have discovered occur frequently in many different types of academic texts. For a complete list of all the Academic Word List words in this chapter and in all the readings in this book, see the Appendix on page 206.

8 eventually	facility	*2* issues	*9* section
6 evident	*4* incidents	physical	*7* transportation
3 excluded	*5* inherently	*10* pursuit	*1* violation

Complete the sentences with words from the list.

1. Many people believed that slavery was a _violation_ of natural law.
2. The candidates for president discussed several important _issues_ during the debate.
3. The language of the Constitution _excluded_ women, Native Americans, and African Americans from voting.
4. Following the Supreme Court ruling, there were many _incidents_ of violence across the South.
5. Poll taxes are _inherent_ unfair because they discriminate against poor people.
6. It soon became _evident_ that some communities would not accept desegregation quickly or easily.
7. Public _transport_ includes buses, trains, and subway systems.
8. Even the communities that opposed desegregation were _eventually_ forced to accept it.
9. The most famous _section_ of King's last speech comes at the end, when he talks about "the promised land."
10. Most immigrants, including the early settlers, came to the United States in _pursuit_ of better opportunities.

Developing Writing Skills

In this section, you will learn to make an outline, which helps you avoid *plagiarizing*, or using an author's words as your own. You will outline your ideas and create a text from the outline in your own words. You will also use what you learn here to complete the writing assignment at the end of this unit.

Making an outline

An important part of successfully expressing ideas in your own words is to develop a good understanding of the text. Outlining helps you understand a text better by helping you analyze the relationships between topics, main ideas, and details. A good outline:

- uses numbers and letters to show how ideas are related;
- includes the most important ideas in the text;
- includes some supporting details.

A In Chapter 5, you learned about the struggle for civil rights. In this section, you will prepare for this writing assignment:

What were the important achievements of the civil rights movement? Review the texts in Chapter 5 and highlight relevant information.

B Discuss these questions in a group. Take notes. Express ideas in your own words. You will use your notes later when you write your outline.

1. What problems did African Americans face in the 50 to 100 years after the Civil War? In other words, what forms of discrimination did they face?
2. What areas of discrimination did the civil rights movement try to change?
3. How did the movement try to change these areas of discrimination?
4. In what areas did the movement succeed or make progress in reducing discrimination?

C Look over your notes from the discussion. Choose **three** topics on civil rights achievements that you think are important. Write them here:

I. _____

II. _____

III. _____

D Consider what you want to say about these topics and organize your ideas.

1. Think about your discussions in Step B. You talked about historical problems and challenges in question 1, and progress and solutions in question 4. Identifying problems and progress in each area (topic) is one way to present a discussion on your three topics.

2. In Unit 2, you used a chart to organize ideas. Now you will use an outline. Make an outline like the one below. Leave lots of space.

> **I.** Topic 1
>   **A.** 1870–1960s – problems
>   **B.** 1960s and later – progress
> **II.** Topic 2
>   **A.** 1870–1960s – problems
>   **B.** 1960s and later – progress
> **III.** Topic 3
>   **A.** 1870–1960s – problems
>   **B.** 1960s and later – progress

E Your outline now has a clear organization but not very much information! Use your discussion notes to fill in facts and ideas. Do not go back to the text. If you do, use your own words to express ideas. The first section has been filled in for you. Notice that these are brief notes, not full sentences. Fill in the rest of the outline.

> **I.** Voting rights
>   **A.** After Civil War – many barriers to voting, for ex. poll taxes, literacy tests, and grandfather laws
>   **B.** 1960s and later – _____
> **II.** _____
>   **A.** 1870–1960s – _____
>   **B.** 1960s and later – _____
> **III.** _____
>   **A.** 1870–1960s – _____
>   **B.** 1960s and later – _____

F Now you have a complete outline. Choose one of the topics and write a paragraph.

- Begin with a topic sentence that makes a claim and says what the paragraph will be about – achievements of the civil rights movement in the topic you chose.
- Write 1–2 sentences on past challenges and problems. Give examples.
- Write 1–2 sentences on how the civil rights movement caused change.

G Exchange papers with a partner. Discuss these questions.

- Does the topic sentence clearly state a claim? How can it be clearer?
- Does the evidence fully support the claim? What other evidence can be included?
- Are there grammar or spelling errors? If so, how can they be corrected?
- Are all ideas stated in your own words?

H Make revisions based on your discussion.

Chapter 6
The Struggle Continues

Understanding key terms Ⓡ Ⓥ

A Read the sentences below. The words in **bold** appear in the reading, "What Does Equality Mean Today?" Use the context to try to understand the meaning of these words.

_d_ **1.** The university's admission policy was **biased** against minority students.

_e_ **2.** Many people believe that hiring decisions should depend only on applicants' **merit**, not on their race or gender.

_b_ **3.** Critics of the government believe there is unequal **access** to educational opportunities in the United States.

_c_ **4.** Equal opportunity does not guarantee equal economic **outcomes**.

_a_ **5.** Everyone should have an equal opportunity to compete for **resources**, such as housing, education, and jobs.

B Look at the definitions below. Match the definitions to the words in bold in Step A. Write the letter in the correct blank.

5 **a.** useful or valuable things (noun)

3 **b.** the right or opportunity to use something or do something (noun)

4 **c.** results or effects (noun)

1 **d.** having an unreasonable preference for or against something or someone (adjective)

2 **e.** good qualities that deserve praise (noun)

C With a partner or in a small group, discuss how _merit_, _access_, and _resources_ could relate to the issue of equality.

Reading 1

WHAT DOES EQUALITY MEAN TODAY?

What does equality mean in American society today? There are several different answers to this question and three basic perspectives. One answer is that there are no differences among Americans; we are all the same. A second idea is somewhat different. It states that we may not
5 all be equal, but all Americans should all have an equal opportunity to compete for resources such as jobs, housing, and education. A third possibility also recognizes differences among Americans, but focuses on equal outcomes. In this last perspective, equal access and opportunity are not enough. Resources, such as jobs and education, should be
10 distributed to ensure all Americans achieve the same level of success.

It seems fairly easy to reject the first somewhat idealistic view. Americans are clearly not all the same. There are differences based on race, ethnicity, social class, gender, religion, and other factors. Examining these second and the third viewpoints is more complicated.

Does equality mean equal opportunity?

15 The second view on the meaning of equality says that we are all different, but none of these differences matters; everyone should have an equal chance
20 to succeed and to compete for resources. This view focuses on providing equal access. In this view, if people are given equal access to resources and
25 opportunities, differences in success are a result of how well they use these opportunities and resources – in other words, differences in merit. Consider
30 an example: If a school with mostly white children has better teachers and equipment than a school with mostly African American children, this will
35 hurt the African American children's chances to succeed, because there is unequal access to resources and opportunities.
This is a problem the government can try to correct by
40 distributing resources more fairly. What if the government provides the two schools with the same resources? What if the African American students attend the school with

mostly white children and better resources? Will that ensure equality? In fact, history suggests that equal opportunity does not always guarantee equal outcomes. To continue the example, providing better resources has not necessarily led to equal success for African Americans. This could be a result of larger problems of social and economic inequality in society. Perhaps the African American children are more likely to be from poor families who cannot give them the support they need to succeed in school. The children may not have a quiet place to study, they may not get healthful meals, or their parents may not have the time or ability to help them with their work. As a result, the children may not be able to benefit fully from the better resources.

Does equality mean equal outcomes?

A third perspective on equality is that there should be equal outcomes. According to this view, the government should ensure that there are not only equal opportunities and resources for minorities but also equal results, that is, that the outcomes should be a more equal share in life, including equal representation in their communities. In examining this view, consider this example from employment: A city police department has a training program and test for officers, but it is biased against women. As a result, few women become police officers. Then the department changes the program and test to be fairer to women, but still few women become officers. The failures could again be a result of broader social conditions. Perhaps the women are afraid to take the test. The women may think they would still not be treated fairly by their bosses or other officers. They may have already experienced some form of discrimination in their jobs. Or, for some other reason, the women do not perform as well as men on the new test. Should the city simply guarantee a certain number of positions in the police department to women?

The answer is yes, from the third perspective. Such policies would correct past discrimination. In addition, and to continue the example, they would create a more diverse and better police force. The diversity, with more women and minorities as police, would better represent the diversity of the community. The goal of these policies is to bring all groups to the same level, that is, to achieve equal outcomes. The same idea applies to education, government, and other activities. However, opponents argue that these policies treat some groups better than other groups and create inequality. The third perspective is controversial because it puts two basic American values in conflict: On the one hand, most Americans believe that everyone deserves an equal opportunity. People who have not had an equal opportunity may deserve some extra help. On the other hand, they believe that hard work and merit – not membership in a specific group – should be the reason one person does well and another person does not. Americans are still trying to find the best ways to ensure equality across society.

Reverse Discrimination

In 1978, Allan Bakke, a white man, claimed that he was the victim of *reverse discrimination*. He argued that he was rejected by a medical school because he was white and that his grades were better than those of African American students who had been accepted.

In the legal case *Bakke versus University of California*, the Supreme Court decided against the medical school and its program that reserved 16 out of 100 places for minority students. The court ordered the university to give Bakke a place in the medical school class.

There have been many challenges to university admission policies since the Bakke case. Current law allows universities to consider race as one of many factors in their admissions decisions. However, even this standard continues to face challenges in the courts. In the *Fisher versus University of Texas* case filed in a lower court in 2008, Abigail Fisher, a white student who was not admitted to the university, has also challenged the university's admission policy and charged the university with reverse discrimination.

Allan Bakke's graduation

1 Reading for main ideas ®

Remember that finding main ideas is your primary task when you read academic texts.

A Read the statements below. Check (✓) the two statements that express the main ideas of the reading.

_____ **1.** Everyone should be treated equally.

✓ **2.** There are different interpretations of what equal treatment means.

_____ **3.** Equal treatment must include some consideration of past discrimination.

_____ **4.** The only fair way to make decisions is based on merit.

✓ **5.** Two important, but quite different, interpretations of equality are equal opportunity and equal outcomes.

_____ **6.** Americans can't decide what equality means, so the Supreme Court has determined what it means.

B Compare answers with a partner.

2 Understanding text structure ⓦ

A text will often contain parts that have different functions, or purposes. These are some common functions.

- To give a definition
- To argue a point of view
- To reject a point of view

Recognizing the function, or purpose, of each part will help you understand the text as a whole.

A Read the list of functions of the paragraphs in the text. Match the functions with the paragraphs. Write the number of the correct paragraph in the blank.

		Par. 2
1. Rejects the view that all Americans are equal		_4_ 3
2. States a third point of view and gives an example		_5_ 3
3. Argues for and against the equal-outcomes view		_3_ 2
4. Explains the equal-opportunity view and poses questions		_1_ 1
5. Defines three points of view on the meaning of equality		

B Study the boxed text. Then with a partner, answer the following questions.

- Which point of view did the University of California take?
- Which point of view did Allan Bakke take?
- Which point of view did Abigail Fisher take?

3 Synonyms Ⓥ

> Authors of academic texts and other writers frequently use synonyms to avoid repetition and to make their writing more interesting.

A Find and highlight each of these words in the text:

> ensure   give   chance   outcomes   view

B Now find a synonym for each word in Step A. Look in the paragraph cited in parentheses. Write the synonym in the blank.

1. ensure (Par. 4) _guarantee_

4. give (Par. 4) _provide_

2. chance (Par. 1) _possibilities_

5. view (Par. 5) _perspective_

3. outcomes (Par. 5) _Resources_

C Add any new words to your vocabulary notebook.

4 Markers of relationship Ⓦ

> Prepositional phrases can be used to mark the type of relationship between facts in a sentence. They can mark a relationship of dependence, of contrast, or of other types.
>
> Three common markers that show dependency are *based on*, *depending on*, and *regardless of*. *Despite/in spite of* stresses a contrast between facts. Here are examples of how each marker is used:
>
> |— X —| |——— Y ———|
> - Discrimination is often **based on** race and gender.
>   (If X is *based on* Y, then Y is a source of/reason for X.)
>
> |—— X ——| |———— Y ————|
> - Choose one of the two topics **depending on** your point of view.
>   (If X will happen *depending on* Y, then X will vary according to what Y is or does.)
>
> |———— X ————| |———— Y ————|
> - Should employers hire employees **regardless of** race and gender?
>   (If X happens *regardless of* Y, this means that Y does not matter. X will happen anyway.)
>
> |——— X ———| |————— Y —————|
> - Many achieved success **despite/in spite of** widespread discrimination.
>   (If X happened *in spite of* Y or *despite* Y means that although Y was a problem or barrier, it did not prevent X from happening.)

A Complete the sentences with a marker of relationship.

1. Everyone should have access to a good education _regardless_ his or her race.
2. The economic success of minority groups varies _based on_ the part of the country in which they live.
3. Most Americans try to get a college education _despite_ its high cost.
4. Unfortunately, some employers make hiring decisions _depending on_ the ethnicity of the applicant.

B Complete the sentences with your own words.

1. His decision was based on _____ .
2. Regardless of your opinion, _____ .
3. Depending on the weather, _____ .
4. He decided to take the job in spite of _____ .

5 Applying what you have read Ⓡ

Read these quotations. Then discuss the questions below in a small group.

> In order to get beyond racism, we must first take into account race. There is no other way. And in order to treat some persons equally, we must treat them differently.
>
> – *Harry Blackmun, Former Supreme Court Justice, 1978*
>
> The way to stop discrimination on the basis of race is to stop discriminating on the basis of race.
>
> – *John Roberts, Chief Justice, Supreme Court, 2007*

1. How can both parts of the last sentence in the Blackmun quote be true? That is, Justice Blackmun believes we must consider race in our treatment of people, but how can people be treated equally and differently?
2. Another way of expressing Justice Roberts's thought is: If we want racial discrimination in our society to end, we must stop making decisions based on race (for example about employment, university admissions). Why do you think he believes this? ·
3. How are these quotations related to the topic of the text you just read?
4. Which of the two Supreme Court justices would favor special treatment for African Americans to correct for past discrimination? Which one would be against it?

1 Predicting ®

Remember that it is a good habit to try to predict the information in a text before you read it. Look at the title, headings, and the first sentence of each paragraph.

Quickly read the following parts of the reading then predict what the reading will be about. Be specific.

- The title
- The headings
- The first sentence of each paragraph

2 Thinking about the topic ®

Work in a small group. Study the photographs below. They show people in places and activities that may be unexpected. Discuss what is unusual and how this could relate to the topic.

Reading 2

EQUAL RIGHTS AND PROTECTION FOR ALL

When we consider prejudice, discrimination, and the fight for equality, we usually think of racial and ethnic minorities. However, other groups have also faced challenges in their struggle for equal rights. Women, the disabled, and older people have all had to fight for laws to
5 protect them against discrimination. Their struggles have resulted in a set of antidiscrimination laws that describe the characteristics that are legally protected. In other words, these laws state that it is illegal to discriminate against people based on specific characteristics, such as race, religion, national origin, gender, age, and disability. These are
10 called *protected classes*. Antidiscrimination laws apply to protected classes in employment, housing, education, health care, and politics.

Gender discrimination

Women were the first to use the strategies that were successful in the civil rights movement: protests, boycotts, and political pressure. As a result, since the 1960s, women have achieved some degree of equality.
15 For example, before the women's movement began, far more men than women attended college. Today, significantly more women than men attend college; the number of men and women attending law, medical, and business schools is almost equal. Women today make up about half of the labor force, and some have become leaders in government
20 and business. By law, employers may no longer discriminate based on gender; in fact, with few exceptions, they may not specify gender or age in job advertisements.

Nevertheless, there is still a gap between men and women, particularly in the workplace. The estimates of the gap vary. For
25 men and women working in the same profession, the gap is smaller. However, according to the U.S. Bureau of Labor Statistics, when comparing all men and women regardless of occupation, women who work full-time earn just 77¢ for every dollar that men with equal experience earn for equal work. For example, on average, if a man
30 earns $100,000 to do a job, a woman receives just $77,000 for the same job. This results in a lifetime difference of $431,000 in wages. Although women make up half of the labor force, 80 percent of them work in job categories that have the lowest pay. There have been many improvements in the status of women, but inequalities remain.
35 Perhaps the most important achievement of the women's movement is that girls who are born today expect an equal chance for success.

Rights for the disabled

It is estimated that more than 50 million Americans – 19 percent of the population – have some form of physical or mental disability,

such as blindness or **depression**. Historically, some people believed
40 that the disabled could not be integrated into society. Therefore, it has
not always been easy for the disabled to gain access to education and
employment. There is a strong relationship between disability and low
income, low levels of education, and unemployment. Over the past
40 years, people with disabilities have fought for equal protection and
45 treatment. Their battle has been difficult but has had positive results.
Today, federal and many state laws prohibit companies, governments,
and institutions from discriminating against people with disabilities.

The 1990 Americans with Disabilities Act (ADA) protects people
with disabilities against discrimination in several areas. In employment,
50 it states that if a person with a disability is qualified to do a particular
job, the employer must accommodate that person, that is, the employer
must offer reasonable assistance for that worker. For example, a worker
in a wheelchair might need a special desk. This kind of accommodation
can be expensive, and many employers have resisted these changes in
55 spite of the law.

The ADA also states that public places and transportation must
provide access for people with disabilities so that they can participate
in daily life. For example, buildings must provide accommodations
such as accessible bathrooms and ramps for people in wheelchairs.
60 Buses and trains must also provide access to the disabled. Although
the ADA may seem to be about special treatment for the disabled,
most disabled people would disagree. They argue that it is really
about allowing them to be just like other people: to live independent
and productive lives, to work, to play, and to go to school along with
65 everyone else. In other words, it is about *not* being special.

Age and ageism

Federal law also prohibits discrimination against people because of their age, specifically, against people who are 40 years old or older. This means that employers cannot base decisions about hiring, pay, or promotion on an employee's age. Similarly, a worker cannot be fired
70 because he or she is "too old." Advertisements for jobs cannot specify age as a requirement. This does not mean that ageism – discrimination based on age – does not exist. When the economy is weak, employers often reduce their workforce. They may fire older workers, who often cost employers more than younger workers, without providing a
75 reason. Older workers who lose their jobs, particularly those over 50, generally have more difficulty finding a new job than younger workers. Experts say that age discrimination remains more acceptable in the workplace than discrimination based on race or gender. When employers say they want "fresh ideas" in their business, they often
80 mean they want younger, cheaper workers.

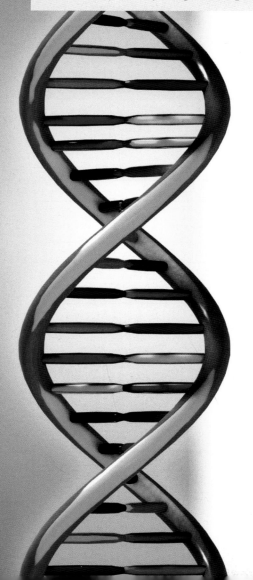

A new protected class

In 2008, GINA, the Genetic Information Non-Discrimination Act, established a new protected class. GINA prohibits discrimination against people based on their genetic information. Genetic information can indicate if a person is likely to become ill in the future. An employer cannot use this information to make decisions about hiring or firing employees. Similarly, an insurance company cannot refuse to insure a person because of his or her genetic history.

1 Reading for details ®

A Look at the three protected classes listed below. For each group, find one detail in the text that shows progress and one detail that shows a continuing challenge. Highlight the details in the text.

- Women
- The disabled
- Older adults

B Do not look at the reading. Rewrite the details in your own words in the blanks below.

Progress P.2
- Women

  Achieve equality to next generation.

- The disabled   P.4

  _____

  _____

- Older adults   7

  _____

  _____

Challenges
- Women   P.3

  _____

  _____

- The disabled   P.4

  _____

  _____

- Older adults   7

  _____

  _____

2 Writing about examples Ⓦ

Examples are often used in academic writing to support main ideas and claims.
Two common expressions for introducing examples are *for example* and *such as*.

for example:	Can introduce a sentence
	Can introduce a noun or a list of nouns but only if the noun or list of nouns is part of a sentence
Correct:	*For example, restaurants must provide accessible bathrooms.*
	A business can provide many types of accommodation for the disabled, for example, ramps, special parking places, and accessible bathrooms.
Incorrect:	*A business can provide many types of accommodation for the disabled.*
	For example, ramps, special parking places, and accessible bathrooms.
such as:	Cannot introduce a sentence
	Can introduce a noun or list of nouns but only if the noun or list of nouns is part of a sentence
Correct:	*A business can provide many types of accommodation for the disabled,* **such as** *ramps and special parking places.*
Incorrect:	*A business can provide many types of accommodation for the disabled, such as they can build ramps and special parking places.*

A Find uses of *for example* and *such as* in the text. Notice the context. Do the uses of these phrases fit the descriptions in the box above?

B Read the sentences with *for example* and *such as*. Check (✓) the correct sentences. Write an *X* by the incorrect sentences.

_X_ **1.** Employers must provide reasonable assistance to disabled workers. Such as they must provide special computers, software, and furniture.

_✓_ **2.** Many older people lose their jobs during bad economic periods, such as the economic downturn of 2008–2009.

_X_ **3.** The ADA has resulted in considerable progress for the disabled. For example, laws against discrimination in education and employment.

_✓_ **4.** Protected classes refer to groups who have experienced discrimination based on certain characteristics, for example, race, sex, or religion.

_X_ **5.** Disabilities are not just physical; they can also be mental. Such as depression.

_✓_ **6.** Employers cannot discriminate in their advertising. For example, they cannot advertise a job specifically for young men.

C Write two sentences about the progress of protected classes in achieving equality. Use *such as* or *for example* in your sentences. Pay attention to where you put the commas.

3 Prepositions with verbs Ⓥ

> Learning prepositions can be difficult. Some prepositions appear with verbs. Sometimes, one preposition can be used with different verbs. Or, one verb can be used with different prepositions. In either case, the meaning of the verb can change depending on the preposition that is used with it. When you learn verbs, be sure to notice and learn the prepositions that often go with them.

A The prepositions in the box appeared in the text with the verbs that follow. Match the prepositions to the verbs. More than one answer may be possible.

against	for	in	on	to

1. to base (a decision, idea) ___on___

2. to discriminate ___against___ someone

3. to participate ___in___ an activity

4. to apply ___to___ a situation

5. to protect someone ___against___ something

6. to struggle ___for / against___ something

7. to fight ___against / for___ something

8. to result ___in___

B Write three sentences about protected classes. Use a verb + preposition combination from Step A for each sentence.

4 Writing about obligations and recommendations Ⓦ

> The modal verb *must* is used to describe necessity. For example, *must* is often used to state or discuss laws and policies. The verb *should* is used to describe obligations and duties, give advice, and make recommendations. *Should* is also used to express what we think is right for people to do or have done.
>
> *Employers **must** provide reasonable accommodation for the disabled.*
>
> *All Americans **must** pay a tax on their income.*
>
> *Tax money **should** be used to support education.*
>
> *Women **should** have the same pay as men for similar work.*

A Review Reading 2 for uses of *must* and highlight them. Study how *must* is used. Then go back to Reading 1 in this chapter and highlight the uses of *should*.

B With a partner, compare how *should* and *must* are used in the two readings.

C Write two statements with *should*. Describe steps that governments, businesses, or other institutions can take to ensure that all citizens are treated equally.

should

1. _____

_____

2. _____

_____

D Write two statements with *must*. Describe the obligations of governments or employers.

must

1. _____

_____

2. _____

_____

5 Applying what you have read ®

A Read the job advertisements – sometimes called "Help Wanted ads" – listed below. Work with a partner. Check (✓) the ads that are legal. Look up unfamiliar words in the dictionary.

1.
Young women needed to answer phones in law office.

2.
Job opportunities for strong, healthy young men with experience in construction.

3.
Position available for experienced restaurant worker.

4.
Help wanted – attractive waitresses in downtown bar.

5.
Great opportunity for new graduates! Must have college degree to apply.

6.
Moving company looking for workers. Must be able to drive a truck.

7.
High-tech firm is now hiring. Looking for college graduates 25–40, for overseas work.

8.
Park service seeks young, healthy employees for outdoor work.

B Discuss the advertisements you did *not* check (✓) with a small group. Explain why they are illegal.

1 Thinking about the topic ⓡ

Work with a partner or a small group to complete the following activities.

A You are going to read a text titled "How Equal Are We Now?" Think of what you have learned in this chapter and describe the state of equality in the United States today. Go back and review the readings if necessary.

B Look at the photographs below. Do these photographs support the ideas you discussed above? Explain.

President Barack Obama

Supreme Court Justice Sonia Sotomayor

Yahoo CEO Marissa Mayer

2 Examining graphics ⓡ

A Look at Figure 6.1 in the reading.

1. What kind of information does it give?
2. For which groups does it provide information?

B Discuss these questions about Figure 6.1 with your partner or group.

1. Look at the top household incomes. Which group appears to be doing the best?
2. Consider the bottom household incomes. Which group seems to be doing the worst?
3. What could be reasons for the differences you noted above?
4. Do these facts change the views you discussed in the previous task? Explain your answer.

Reading 3

HOW EQUAL ARE WE NOW?

The United States and its citizens take pride in their belief in equality. Most Americans believe their country is an egalitarian society, that is, a society of equals. Americans say they judge others based on their individual merit, not their background. In many ways, Americans
5 are much more equal now than in the past. Yet there is a large gap between the rich and poor, and often this gap is related to differences of race or ethnicity. So are all Americans really equal today? How can equality be measured?

The government and many private organizations use statistics to
10 show progress. They also use them to compare population groups within the country, specifically whites and the two largest minorities: African Americans and Latinos. On educational and economic measures, African Americans and Latinos have historically been lower than whites. These minority groups are also not as well represented in government.
15 Statistics from the 2010 census suggest that African Americans and Latinos have made significant progress in some areas. However, there are still ways in which they continue to fall behind the white population.

Education

African Americans have shown a steady increase in high school graduation rates and college attendance. In 1940, only 7 percent of
20 all African Americans finished high school. Census reports show that this figure grew to 51 percent by 1980 and to 84 percent in 2010. However, this rate is still somewhat lower than the 88 percent average for whites. The number of African Americans with a college degree has also risen, from 8 percent in 1980 to 19 percent in 2010;
25 again, this is lower than the 30 percent rate for whites. The figures for Latinos have also shown improvement but remain lower than the African American figures. This may be associated with the challenge of studying in a second language. According to the 2010 census, only 63 percent of Latino adults have completed high school, up from 32
30 percent in 1970, and less than 14 percent have graduated from college, up from 4.5 percent in 1970. In general, throughout the country, poor urban neighborhoods, particularly, tend to have poor schools and insufficient resources. The difference between the educational levels of whites and minorities may be linked to the kinds of schools that
35 each group attends. Public schools in African American and Latino neighborhoods serve more students than public schools in white neighborhoods and have fewer resources.

Economics

The **economic profile** for minorities is also mixed. The **median income** for all minorities has risen substantially in the last 50 years
40 (see Figure 6.1), and fewer minorities live in poverty. Yet according to

economic profile
a description that includes the most important economic facts, such as income and employment

median income the middle point of the income distribution, where half of the population earns more and half of the population earns less

the 2010 census, the poverty rate for minorities remains considerably higher than for whites. About 36 percent of the African American population and 35 percent of the Latino population live in poverty, compared to 14 percent of the white population. Unemployment
45 figures also show considerable differences; minority workers are two to three times more likely to be unemployed than white workers. This contributes to higher poverty levels.

Income levels differ significantly partly because white and minority populations tend to have different **employment profiles**. There is a higher
50 percentage of whites in high-paying professional jobs, such as managers, doctors, and lawyers, and a higher percentage of minority workers in low-paying jobs. These differences in employment and occupation have important consequences. Low-paying jobs are less likely to include benefits such as health insurance. As a result, workers in low-paying
55 jobs may not have access to good health care. These workers may also find it more difficult to save money for important purchases such as a home. Although home ownership by minorities has increased – in 2010, it reached 45 percent for African Americans and 48 percent for Latinos – this figure is still far below the figure for the white population, 74 percent.

employment profile a description of the range of jobs that are typical for a specific group

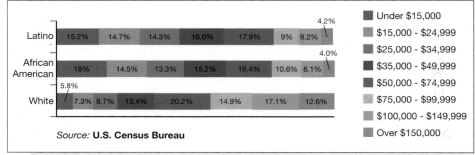

Figure 6.1 Household income – 2010

Representation in government

60 Finally, in a more positive trend, there have been substantial increases in minority representation in the government. The most famous example is Barack Obama, an African American, who became president in 2008. In the past, many African Americans were prevented from voting. In 2012, there were more than 600 black mayors of
65 cities with populations of more than 40,000, 45 black representatives in Congress, and two black governors, but no black senators. There were 25 Latino representatives, two Latino senators, and two Latino governors. These represent significant increases since the end of the twentieth century. African Americans and Latinos have been in an
70 increasing number of important and powerful appointed positions, including the Attorney General and other cabinet positions. In 2009, Obama appointed the first Latino Supreme Court justice, Sonia Sotomayor. While the struggle for equality continues, Americans are closer to being equal now than in the past.

Minorities have also increased their visibility in the media and the arts. Oprah Winfrey is a famous businesswoman, talk show host, and actress. She was born in a poor family in Mississippi. She had a very difficult childhood but got a good education and began a career in television. For 25 years (1986–2011), she had one of the country's most popular television programs. She now runs a huge communication company. She is the richest African American and the only African American billionaire. Because of her considerable influence on popular opinion, *CNN* and *Time Magazine* have called her the world's most powerful woman.

1 Reading about statistics Ⓡ Ⓐ

Academic texts often use statistics as supporting evidence. If a text has many statistics, it is a good idea to organize them in your notes in some way. You might use a chart or a graph, which will show the relationships and patterns in them. This will help you understand the statistics and how they relate to the text. It will also help you prepare for writing assignments and tests.

A Fill in the chart with facts from the text. (Note: The text does not provide information for all of the boxes.)

	Percent that . . .	1970	1980	2010
African Americans	graduated from college		8	19
	lived in poverty			36
	owned a home			45
	had a household income above $150,000			40
Latinos	graduated from college	4.5		14
	lived in poverty			35
	owned a home			48
	had a household income above $150,000			42
Whites	graduated from college			30
	lived in poverty			14
	owned a home			44
	had a household income above $150,000			12.6

B Now discuss these questions with a partner.

1. Do these statistics show significant progress in achieving equality?

2. Do you think the progress will continue?

2 Writing about statistics Ⓦ

Statistical information is often reported in academic writing along with the name of the source. Sometimes, however, sources are not named within the text if the information is well known or the source itself is not as important as the statistic. In these cases, it is common to use a passive verb to present the information. One verb that is frequently used in the passive to report statistics is *estimate*.

*The population of the United States **was estimated** to be more than 310,000,000 in 2012.*

***It is estimated** that more than 200,000 people died in the 2004 tsunami.*

A Read these sentences from texts in this book.

It is **estimated that** more than two-thirds of the original 300 native languages are dead or dying.

As a result, the number of Mexicans crossing the border illegally **is now estimated to be** about 150,000 per year.

It is estimated that 5.2 percent of the American workforce is undocumented.

B Using the information in Figure 6.1, write two sentences with the passive construction *it is estimated that X* or *X is estimated to be*.

3 Synonyms Ⓥ

A Find synonyms in the text for the words and phrases below. The paragraph number where you will find the synonym appears before the blank. Some synonyms appear more than once. Pay attention to the word form you need.

1. big / bigger
   (Par. 1) _large_
   (Par. 4) _considerable_
   (Par. 6) _substantial_

2. a lot (adv)
   (Par. 4) _substantially_
   (Par. 4) _considerably_

3. is connected to
   (Par. 1) _related to_
   (Par. 3) _associated with_
   (Par. 3) _linked to_

B Using two of the synonyms from Step A, write two sentences of your own that describe the trends presented in the text.

C Add any new words to your vocabulary notebook.

4 Reviewing for a test Ⓐ

Reviewing the text with a classmate can deepen your understanding of the material and help you prepare for a test.

A Work with a partner. Answer and discuss these questions. Do not look back at the texts in this unit.

1. What are some different perspectives on the meaning of equality?
2. What can the government do to promote equality?
3. What is a protected class? Give some examples.
4. How is (in)equality measured? Give some examples.
5. What kinds of progress have different protected classes made toward equality?
6. Where does inequality still exist in American society?

B Look back at the texts to check your answers.

Chapter 6 Academic Vocabulary Review

The following words appear in the readings in Chapter 6. They all come from the Academic Word List, a list of words that researchers have discovered occur frequently in many different types of academic texts. For a complete list of all the Academic Word List words in this chapter and in all the readings in this book, see the Appendix on page 206.

a, on the next – main

accommodate	3 distribute	occupation	8 purchases
5 achieve	9 integrate	1 perspectives (n)	6 status
7 benefits	4 media	10 promotion	2 visibility

Complete the sentences with words from the lists.

1. During the 1950s and 1960s, people in different parts of the country had very different _____ on civil rights.

2. The election of Barack Obama has increased the _____ of African Americans in government.

3. One of the functions of government is to collect money in taxes and then _____ these resources to people who need them.

4. Television, radio, newspapers, and the Internet are the major types of _____ today.

5. Most people want others to judge them based on what they _____ , not on what groups they belong to.

6. The economic _____ of minority groups in the United States has improved considerably.

7. Many immigrants want to enjoy the _____ of citizenship, such as the right to vote.

8. The two biggest _____ that most families want to make are a house and a car.

9. Immigrants who are white and look like European Americans have usually found it easier to _____ into American society than immigrants who look different.

10. After working at the company for eight years, she was hoping for a _____ to a better position.

Practicing
Academic Writing

In this unit, you have learned about the fight for equal rights and about protected groups. You will write two paragraphs based on what you have learned. You will also use the pre-writing skills you learned in Developing Writing Skills in Chapter 5.

Leveling the playing field

"Leveling the playing field" means that no person or group should have an unfair advantage. You will write two paragraphs on equal rights and equal protection, giving your perspective on the treatment of protected groups. You will need to decide what equality means for these groups.

PREPARING TO WRITE

Think about the title of your assignment, "Leveling the playing field," which is an expression from sports. *Leveling* means "making something flat and even." The expression refers to the idea that a game should be fair; the winner should be the person or the team who plays better. One team should not have a better field, better equipment, or better clothes; none of these should be a factor in victory. The same expression is used outside of sports. It refers to the idea that, like a team, no group should have an unfair advantage. Similarly, no group of people should have a disadvantage before they even begin (school, a job, etc.).

A Work with a group. Discuss the expression, "leveling the playing field." Are there similar expressions in your own language? Explain them to your classmates.

B The first text in Chapter 6, "What Does Equality Mean Today?" presented the following important, but different, perspectives on the meaning of equality in the United States. Read this summary of these two views:

A **second** idea is somewhat different. It states that we may not all be equal, but all Americans should all have an equal opportunity to compete for resources such as jobs, housing, and education. A **third** possibility also recognizes differences among Americans but focuses on equal outcomes. In this last perspective, equal access and opportunity is not enough. Resources, such as jobs and education, should be distributed to ensure all Americans achieve the same level of success.

You considered how two Supreme Court justices viewed these two perspectives. Now it is your turn to offer your ideas. In a small group, prepare by discussing the following questions. Take notes on your discussion.

1. What do *you* think equality means?

2. Should society promote equality for all? How can this be achieved?

3. Consider protected groups. Do they have a "level playing field"? Discuss specific ways that they do or don't. Then answer this question: Should some groups, but not others, receive special help in order to help them achieve equality? Or should all receive the same treatment or no special treatment? Why or why not?

4. If you believe the playing field is *not* equal and that some groups do need extra assistance, what should that assistance be? For which groups?

C Now you must decide on your own perspective. Consider the three perspectives on equality. Read each one carefully. Check (✓) the one you agree with.

_____ **Perspective 1.** Everyone, including protected groups, should have equal access and opportunity; differences in success are due to merit or what we do with our opportunities and access. (This is the **second** view on equality given in Reading 1 and included in the summary in Step B above.)

_____ **Perspective 2.** Equal access and opportunity are not enough for some protected groups. To help them overcome the disadvantages of past discrimination, we should give them extra assistance, including some certain guarantees of representation in education and the workplace. This stronger action can also create diversity that better reflects the communities in which they live. (This is the **third** idea about equality given in Reading 1 and included in the summary in Step B above.)

_____ **Perspective 3.** Some groups do have particular disadvantages. For this reason, society owes them extra assistance in order to help them achieve equality. On the other hand, there are other protected groups that do not need this extra help. If they have equal access and opportunity, they should be able to achieve equality without it. (This is a combination of the two perspectives.)

D Make an outline for your paragraphs, as you did in Developing Writing Skills in Chapter 5. You may want to review that section.

The first paragraph will be the same regardless of your choice in Step C. That is, it must include your point of view and the reasons for it. However, the second paragraph will vary depending on your perspective, that is, depending on your choice in Step C. Read the outline on page 151 and choose one option for your second paragraph. You may include more details than the ones that are shown in the outline.

I. Statement of your point of view

    A. Give a reason.

    B. Give a second reason.

II. Special treatment or assistance

    Perspective 1

    A. Suggest examples of special treatment.

    B. Give a reason why these are not appropriate or a good idea.

    C. Give another reason why these are not appropriate or a good idea.

    Perspective 2

    A. State the need for special treatment for protected classes.

    B. Give an example of special treatment.

    C. Give reasons why special treatment is an appropriate choice or a good idea.

    Perspective 3

    A. State the need for special treatment for some protected classes but not for other classes.

    B. Give an example of this special treatment.

    C. Give a reason why this special treatment is an appropriate choice or a good idea for one protected group.

    D. Give a reason why this special treatment is not appropriate for another protected group.

E Use the outline to organize your material and to write short notes about your ideas. Be careful to use your own words when you write your notes. Fill in your outline with facts and information that you have learned in this unit. Be sure to use your own words.

NOW WRITE

A Write your first paragraph.

1. Begin with your introduction. Help your reader understand what you are going to write about. Use these two steps to accomplish this.

- Give background. Write one or two sentences that will educate the reader about the issue of equality. You have now read a lot about equality and how it can be achieved, but your reader may not know anything about this subject. Make these sentences general. Here are some possible ways to begin:

  Equality is a very complicated . . .

  Both the government and the public have been trying to . . .

  Throughout U.S. history, . . .

- Include a statement that will explain the information in both paragraphs. That is, write a clear statement of *your* perspective: 1, 2, or 3. You may wish to use the expression that you discussed in Preparing to Write: "Leveling the playing field."

Remember not to add *I think, I believe,* or *my opinion is* when you state your point of view. In academic writing, the statement is your point of view.

2. Finish your first paragraph using the information in your outline.

B Now write your second paragraph.

1. Write a topic sentence. It should cover the information in this paragraph. Remember that a topic sentence:
   - states what the paragraph will be about (special treatment); and
   - makes a claim or says something interesting about the topic of the paragraph.

2. Review the examples and reasons in your outline for paragraph 2 and then write the rest of the paragraph to support the claim you made in your topic sentence.

   Review the use of *must* and *should* on page 140. Remember that *must* is often used to describe laws and policies, and *should* is used to give advice and make recommendations. Which is appropriate for this paragraph?

C Reread your paper and make sure that you have included the required elements. Check for grammar and spelling errors.

AFTER YOU WRITE

A Reread your own paragraphs. Check that:

- the first paragraph begins by telling the reader about the issue of equality;
- the first paragraph contains a clear statement of your point of view;
- the second paragraph has a topic sentence about special treatment; and
- both of your paragraphs contain support for the claims you have made and for your point of view stated in the first paragraph.

B Exchange papers with a partner. Discuss the following questions about your paragraphs:

- Does the first sentence provide some explanation of the topic?
- Has your partner written good topic sentences for each paragraph?
- Has your partner given appropriate, clear reasons for his or her point of view (Par. 1)?
- Has your partner given appropriate, clear examples of special treatment and reasons that it should or should not be provided (Par. 2)?

C Revise your work. Use your partner's suggestions and your own ideas.

D Edit your paragraphs.

- Look for errors in spelling and grammar.
- Make corrections whenever you find errors.

Unit 4
American Values

In this unit, you will look at some of the basic values that are the foundation of much of American social, economic, and political life. In Chapter 7, you will explore the origins of these values and see how they are connected to the development of business. You will also explore Americans' continuing romantic views of life on the frontier. In Chapter 8, you will consider how these values are reflected in contemporary American life at home and on the road, and examine the roots and future of an idea that is often referred to as "the American Dream."

Contents

In Unit 4, you will read and write about the following topics.

Chapter 7 A History of American Values	Chapter 8 American Values Today
Reading 1 The Roots of American Values **Reading 2** The American West **Reading 3** The Business of Success	**Reading 1** The Individual and Society: Rights and Responsibilities **Reading 2** The Open Road and Car Culture **Reading 3** Is the American Dream Still Possible?

Skills

In Unit 4, you will practice the following skills.

R **Reading Skills**	**W** **Writing Skills**
Increasing reading speed Applying what you have read Previewing art Reading for details Examining graphics Thinking about the topic Predicting Understanding cartoons Reading for main ideas Scanning Reading actively	Noun + infinitive phrases *Few* and *a few* Writing about change Understanding text structure Writing about reasons Gerunds Writing definitions
V **Vocabulary Skills**	**A** **Academic Success Skills**
Understanding key terms Word families Collocations Prepositions	Preparing for a test Answering multiple-choice questions Responding to a quote Answering true/false questions Conducting a survey

Learning Outcomes

Write a four-paragraph essay on American values

Previewing the Unit

Before reading a unit (or chapter) in a textbook, it is a good idea to preview the contents page and think about the topics that will be covered. This will help you understand how the unit is organized and what it is going to be about.

Read the contents page for Unit 4 on page 154 and do the following activities.

Chapter 7: A History of American Values

In this chapter you are going to read about some traditional American values in business and in everyday life.

A At the end of the nineteenth century, the United States was on its way to becoming the most powerful nation in the world. Look at the pictures below. What do you see? What values might these scenes suggest?

B Consider the texts that you have read and the pictures above of the United States in the nineteenth century. Then discuss the following question with a group of classmates: What was responsible for the United States' success?

Chapter 8: American Values Today

In this chapter, you are going to learn how some traditional American values are connected to life in the United States today.

A Read this list of generalizations that have been made about the United States and Americans.

- The United States is a land of opportunity, where anyone can succeed.
- Americans believe in hard work.
- Your family background is not important in the United States.
- Everything moves fast in the United States; you have to move fast, too.
- Everyone is equal in the United States.

B Work with a partner or small group and discuss these questions.

1. Have you heard these generalizations before? If so, which ones have you heard?
2. Do you think some of these generalizations are true? Which ones? Why or why not?

Chapter 7
A History of American Values

Increasing reading speed ®

A Review the strategies for increasing your reading speed on page 77.

B Read "The Roots of American Values," using the strategies.

1. Before you begin, enter your starting time: _____
2. After you finish, enter your finishing time: _____

C Calculate your reading speed.

Number of words in the text (785) ÷

Number of minutes it took you to read the text =

Reading speed _____

Your goal should be about 150–180 words per minute.

D Check your reading comprehension. Answer these questions. Do not look at the text.

1. Check (✓) the items that are basic American values according to the text.

    _____ **a.** hard work

    _____ **b.** the importance of religion

    _____ **c.** the importance of your family's position in society

    _____ **d.** self-reliance

    _____ **e.** individual rights

    _____ **f.** self-discipline

    _____ **g.** the belief that good things will happen

    _____ **h.** the equality of all individuals

    _____ **i.** the importance of money

2. Read the statements about the text. Write *T* (true) or *F* (false) for each statement.

    _____ **a.** The authors of the Declaration of Independence and the Constitution got their ideas for these documents from European traditions.

    _____ **b.** In its early days, the United States did not have a strong class system.

    _____ **c.** The settlers who came to the United States saw endless natural resources.

    _____ **d.** The values that the text discusses are only American. People from other countries do not share these values.

Reading 1

THE ROOTS OF AMERICAN VALUES

There are consistent themes in many areas of social and political life in the United States as well as in the personal behavior and attitudes of its citizens. These themes are a reflection of fundamental American values. These values, which have their origins in the early history
5 of the country and the people who settled it, fall into four basic categories. First, Americans have a deep belief in the basic equality of all individuals. They believe that all people should have an equal chance to succeed and that everyone should have an equal say in what happens in their country. Indeed, this is at the root of the American
10 idea of democracy. Along with this belief in equality, Americans strongly value hard work, ambition, and self-reliance. Related to this idea is the basic value of individualism: a belief in the power of individuals to control their own lives. Traditionally, Americans have believed that their success depends on their own decisions and
15 efforts, not on luck or their connections to people with power. Finally, Americans are optimistic. They believe they can improve their own lives but also that they can make the world a better place. They are willing to take risks to do so.

Certainly, these values are not exclusively American, but there
20 are historical reasons for the presence of these consistent themes in American society, and they have consequences in public and private life. The founders of the nation, the men who wrote the Declaration of Independence and the Constitution, put their egalitarian beliefs into these documents. They believed in the fundamental equality of
25 all men and that individuals should be judged by their achievements. At that time in Europe, family background and class were more important than individual achievement. If you were from an upper-class family, your world was secure and comfortable; if you were poor, you had little chance of success. The men who established the
30 nation's first government wanted the United States to be different. This belief that the United States is in some way exceptional and that it has special responsibilities or a special place in the world has persisted in the imagination of many Americans.

In the New World, settlers founded a society without a strong
35 class system that would limit their dreams. They believed the only limit on their dreams was their own ambition and effort. Many of the first settlers were Protestants, who shared a belief in the power of hard work and self-discipline. They believed these were ways of improving themselves in the eyes of God, who would reward them
40 for this discipline. This attitude toward life is sometimes referred to as the "Protestant work ethic." However, this attitude was shared by immigrants of many different backgrounds and religions. All of them were eager to work hard to achieve success in their new country.

The combination of these two values has important implications: If you believe that you are as good as anyone else and that you can succeed as a result of your own efforts, you are also likely to believe that you have the ability to control your own future. In the eighteenth century, this belief in the power and importance of individuals – referred to as *individualism* – was not common. Many people believed that they had little control over their own lives. The rebellion against this perspective was apparent in many aspects of Americans' lives, in their desire to make their own choices, their wish for privacy, and their wish for others, including the government, to stay out of their lives.

Finally, the settlers came to a land that seemed to have endless resources. There were forests full of wood, rich lands for farming, and abundant animal life for hunting. Later, they found gold, silver, and other minerals under the ground. This natural wealth encouraged the optimism of early Americans and made them feel confident of success in their new country.

All of these circumstances came together to make American society different from the societies that preceded it. Because of their faith in the basic equality of all human beings and the equality of opportunity in America, the early settlers and the founders of the country believed that individuals could and should control their own lives. This idea – that with hard work and courage, all people can achieve success – is often called "the American Dream." This view has positive and negative implications. On one hand, Americans believe that individuals are responsible for their own success; on the other hand, they also tend to believe that those who fail have not worked hard enough. However, they don't see failure as an end; there is always a second chance and a way forward if you keep trying.

1 Preparing for a test Ⓐ

Taking notes can help you prepare for a test. You have learned different ways to take notes, including highlighting, making a chart, and making an outline. There is no one right way to take notes; you should choose a way that works best for you. Here are some guidelines for using notes to prepare for a test.

- Take notes using a method of your choice. Remember that you can use a variety of methods for the same text.
- Review your notes and decide how the information could be organized into central themes or points.
- In a separate document, organize the information in your notes in the themes you have chosen.
- Use your organized notes to predict test questions.

A Skim the reading and consider how to take notes on the text. Can you chart key ideas with dates and descriptions? Can you outline or highlight major and minor details?

B Reread the text carefully and take notes. Use one or more of the techniques that you have learned.

C Review your notes and organize the information into themes or main ideas. Some themes that you might use for this text are listed below. You may decide to add others.

- Belief in equality
- Work ethic
- Individualism
- Abundant resources and optimism
- "The American Dream"

D Now use your notes to predict test questions.

1. For each of your themes, predict one test question. Use a variety of question types. (Review "Understanding Test Questions" on page 44 if necessary.)
2. Exchange questions with a partner, and give an oral response to your partner's questions.
3. Compare your questions in a small group. If your questions were similar, you probably did a good job of predicting test questions.

2 Understanding key terms Ⓥ

A Match the key terms with their definitions. Write the correct letter in the blank.

_____ 1. values

_____ 2. risks

_____ 3. self-discipline

_____ 4. individualism

_____ 5. egalitarianism

_____ 6. self-reliance

_____ 7. optimism

_____ 8. ambition

a. the ability to make yourself do things that you should do even when you don't want to do them

b. hopefulness and belief that good things will happen

c. the strong desire to become powerful or successful at something

d. beliefs about what is right and wrong and what is important in life

e. actions or situations that might turn out badly

f. the belief that all people are equally important

g. the belief in the importance of the individual and personal independence

h. the ability to succeed without the help or support of others

B Complete the sentences. Use the key terms from Step A.

1. The settlers were famous for their _____ . They lived alone in the wilderness and rarely asked for help from their neighbors.

2. The men who wrote the Constitution supported _____ , that is, the fundamental equality of all men.

3. Many new Americans had to take _____ in their efforts to make a new life. Some found success; some failed.

4. The immigrants who came to the United States were filled with _____ about starting a new life in a new country.

5. An important element in the success of many business and political leaders is their strong _____ . They have a powerful desire to succeed.

6. Many Americans believe that hard work and _____ are the keys to success. Many new Americans have done work they do not like in order to succeed.

7. Americans' belief in _____ means they think people should make their own choices. It also means that each person's independence is very important.

8. _____ such as hard work and self-discipline were especially typical of the Christians who were the majority in the first waves of immigrants.

3 Noun + infinitive phrases Ⓦ

Phrases that include the noun/noun phrase + infinitive form are very common in academic writing. When infinitives are linked with certain nouns, they can be used to express goals, opportunities, and abilities, for example:

noun   infinitive

Immigrants had *a chance to start* new lives.

noun phrase   infinitive

The protesters fought for *the right of all citizens to vote*.

Nouns that are frequently used with infinitives include:

(in)ability	desire	opportunity	responsibility
attempt	effort	power	right
chance	need	refusal	wish

A Find one noun/noun phrase + infinitive form in these paragraphs in the text. Circle the noun or noun phrase and underline the infinitive.

1. Paragraph 1
2. Paragraph 1
3. Paragraph 4
4. Paragraph 4

B Read the sentences. Find the noun/noun phrase + infinitive form. Circle the noun and underline the infinitive.

1. All people should have an equal chance to succeed.
2. The Constitution gives Congress the power to create courts.
3. It seemed to be a land of endless opportunity for someone with a good idea and the willingness to take a risk.
4. A fundamental value is the right of individuals to make their own decisions.
5. Many settlers believed it was their destiny to populate the land from one coast to the other.
6. Native Americans believed they had a responsibility to care for the land.

C Choose two of the nouns listed below and use each in a sentence about the United States, Americans, or American culture or history. Use noun + infinitive phrases in your sentences.

ability	duty	responsibility
chance	effort	right

1. _____

_____

2. _____

_____

4 Applying what you have read ®

Proverbs and sayings illustrate basic values and ways of behaving in a culture. Understanding the proverbs of a culture can deepen your understanding of that culture.

A Discuss the meaning of these proverbs with your classmates. Look up words you don't know.

_____ **1.** The early bird gets the worm.

_____ **2.** God helps those who help themselves.

_____ **3.** Idle hands are the devil's workshop.

_____ **4.** The show must go on.

_____ **5.** If at first you don't succeed, try, try again.

_____ **6.** Today is the first day of the rest of your life.

_____ **7.** There is no free lunch.

_____ **8.** Little strokes fell mighty oaks.

_____ **9.** If life hands you lemons, make lemonade.

_____ **10.** Where there's a will, there's a way.

B Read these descriptions of values. Match the values to the proverbs in Step A. Write the letter of the value in the correct blank above. Some proverbs may illustrate more than one value.

a. the importance of hard work and discipline

b. the importance of continuing to try even though there are challenges and problems

c. the need for independence and self-reliance

d. optimism about the future

C Discuss similar proverbs that you know from other cultures. What values do they illustrate?

1 Previewing art Ⓡ

A Look at the pictures on the right and on pages 164–165.

B Discuss these questions in a small group.

   1. What do these pictures make you think of?

   2. Which pictures do you think show what life was really like in the old American West? Explain your answer.

   3. Have you seen films or television programs that use similar images?

   4. There are many films, television programs, and books about the American West. Why do you think there are so many?

2 Understanding key terms Ⓥ

A Read the sentences using vocabulary from the text. Match the **bold** words with their definitions on the right. Write each word in the correct blank. Note that some definitions are specific to the usage in the text.

The **pioneers** left their towns in the East and began to move west, where the country was still wild.

   1. a border between developed land where white people live and undeveloped land where Native Americans live _____

Many Native American tribes were forced to **cede** their land to the U.S. government.

   2. an idea that is incorrect but that many people believe is true _____

At first, only a few white people lived on the western **frontier**.

   3. people who are among the first to do something _____

The pioneers believed it was their **destiny** to develop and live on the new land.

   4. events that are going to happen in the future; events that no one can control _____

The pioneers built homes in the **wilderness**, which was full of forests and animals.

   5. land that has not been farmed or developed _____

The idea of the western frontier is part **myth** and part truth.

   6. to give something away unwillingly _____

B Add any new words to your vocabulary notebook.

Reading 2

THE AMERICAN WEST

Few images have as powerful a place in the American imagination as the symbols of the American West, such as the covered wagon, the log cabin, and the cowboy. Why are they so powerful? One reason is that these images of the West are deeply connected with traditional values, 5 such as self-reliance and hard work, which many Americans believe give their nation strength and character. However, it is important to note that the idea of the western frontier is partly a myth; it includes what Americans want to believe happened. What really happened as Americans moved west was not always what they would like to 10 remember.

Large numbers of pioneers from Europe and the eastern part of the United States began moving west in the nineteenth century. Between1841 and 1866, half a million people moved west. For these people, the West, which meant land west of the Mississippi River, seemed to be a place 15 of unlimited opportunity and resources: excellent farmland and land rich in minerals, thick forests, and plenty of animals for hunting. The land and the sky seemed to stretch without end, waiting for them. Many people moved west to get away from cities and overcrowded urban areas. They dreamed of being free of civilization and of living in open places.

A home in the West around 1900

However, this search for a new life had a cost. The westward journey
and life in the West were dangerous and difficult. There were many
physical hardships and few comforts or conveniences on the western
trails. While many American movies portray the hardships, they
often show the pioneers winning against the odds of survival. In fact,
however, there were many who did not win. About 40,000 people died
along the western trails from illness, hunger, and cold. One of them, the
Oregon Trail, has been called the nation's longest graveyard. Only the
toughest and most self-reliant pioneers did well in these circumstances.
They had to be able to build houses for themselves, farm, raise
animals, hunt for food, and protect themselves and their property. A
final important characteristic of the frontier was its social equality. In
the struggle to survive, success depended on the pioneers' individual
strength and resourcefulness, not on money or family background.

Throughout the nineteenth century,
the pioneers moved west, and their
journeys brought harsh consequences
of other kinds. The pioneers and
the American government believed
it was the destiny of Americans to
populate the land from one coast
to the other. They believed they
were bringing civilization to the
wilderness. However, this movement
westward – often called the **westward
expansion** – contributed to the deaths
of thousands of Native Americans
and the destruction of many native
communities. Furthermore, as more
people moved west, the frontier became
less and less like the wilderness of their
dreams, and more and more like the
communities they had left back in the
East.

"Death Scene on the Plains"

Over time, much of the reality of the pioneer experience was
forgotten in the American imagination, while a more romantic picture
of the old West, a narrower view, took shape: the strong, silent cowboy,
tough and independent pioneers, with wide open spaces and freedom
and endless opportunity. This is the frontier myth that has been kept
alive in American culture, in many books, art, movies, and advertising
about the Old West.

**westward
expansion** the
movement of settlers
to the western
United States in the
nineteenth century

Acquisition of new land for a new nation

At the end of the War of Independence, England ceded the United States all of its territory east of the Mississippi River. During the next hundred years, the new country acquired all of the land between the Mississippi and the Pacific Ocean. The American government accomplished this in several different ways. It bought the land (for example, Alaska), it simply took the land – this is called *annexation* (for example, Indian territories), or it acquired the land in a treaty or war (for example, California). When one country loses a war, it often must cede its land. In some cases, the government acquired the land through a combination of these methods (Texas, for example, whose annexation started with a war). The map shows when different areas of the country were added. Below is a list of what the government paid for some of these purchases.

Louisiana Purchase (1803) – $15 million

Mexican Cession (1848) – $15 million

Gadsden Purchase (1853) – $10 million

Alaska Purchase (1867) – $7.2 million

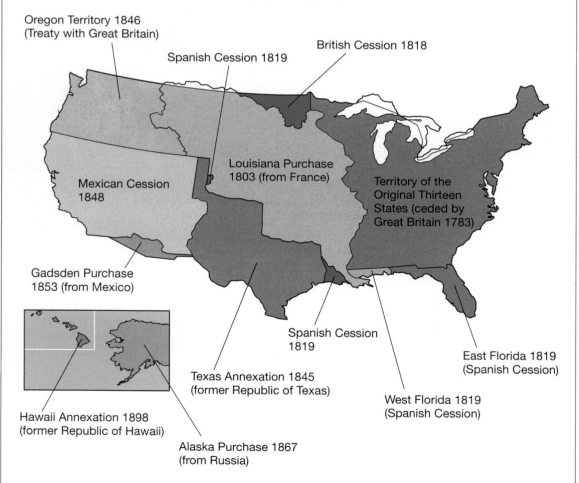

U.S. territorial acquisitions

Oregon Territory 1846
(Treaty with Great Britain)

Spanish Cession 1819

British Cession 1818

Mexican Cession
1848

Louisiana Purchase
1803 (from France)

Territory of the
Original Thirteen
States (ceded by
Great Britain 1783)

Gadsden Purchase
1853 (from Mexico)

Spanish Cession
1819

East Florida 1819
(Spanish Cession)

Texas Annexation 1845
(former Republic of Texas)

West Florida 1819
(Spanish Cession)

Hawaii Annexation 1898
(former Republic of Hawaii)

Alaska Purchase 1867
(from Russia)

1 Reading for details ®

Many academic assignments ask you to look for evidence in a new text that supports ideas you have read about in previous assignments.

A Review the values that you learned about in "The Roots of American Values," on pages 157–158.

B Highlight evidence in "The American West" that supports each of the values below. Use a different color for each value if possible.

- Self-reliance
- Optimism
- Taking risks
- Egalitarianism

2 Examining graphics ®

A Review the map on page 166 and the information in the boxed text.

B Work with a partner and answer the following questions.

1. How did the U.S. acquire most of its land? Order the methods 1–4 as they are discussed in the boxed text. Write the correct number in the blank.
   a. _____ annexation
   b. _____ cession or treaty with another country
   c. _____ purchase
   d. _____ combination

2. The map does not mention Native American land. How were Native American lands acquired?

3. Today it seems that the government paid very little for the land purchases. What would they have to pay today for the Louisiana Purchase? Check (✓) your guess! Then check your answer below.
   _____ **a.** about $150,000 million
   _____ **b.** about $250,000 million
   _____ **c.** about $1 billion

Answer to Examining graphics, number 3:b.

3 Few and a few Ⓦ

> Few and a few are both ways of describing quantities. However, their meanings can be different.
>
> few = not many or not enough
>
>   **Few** pioneers could read or write well.
>
>   **Few** things are more important than freedom.
>
> a few = some; a small number of
>
>   Immigrants brought **a few** valued possessions for their journey across the ocean.
>
>   The government established **a few** military posts west of the Mississippi.

A The word *few* appears in two sentences in "The American West." Scan the text to find the word each time it appears and highlight it.

B Work with a partner and answer the following question about the sentences you highlighted in Step A. Is its meaning closer to "not many/not enough," or is it closer to "some"? What clues helped you decide?

C Discuss the difference in meaning between the sentences below. What clues helped you decide?

 1. Scholars were disappointed to learn that **few** photographs of the western expansion have survived.

 2. Scholars were excited to learn that **a few** photographs of the western expansion have survived.

D Complete the sentences with *few* or *a few*.

 1. There are _____ symbols that seem more American than the cowboy.

 2. You can still visit _____ places in the American West where there is wilderness.

 3. The American pioneers had to depend on their families and _____ neighbors for help in emergencies.

 4. Life in the new western settlements offered many resources but _____ comforts or conveniences.

4 Word families ⓥ

> One way to figure out the meaning of an unknown word is to think of other words in the same word family that you already know. For example, you may be able to figure out the meaning of *wilderness* if you know the meaning of *wild*. Even if you cannot figure out the exact meaning, you can understand enough to continue reading.

A Look at the phrases from the text. Write down at least one other word you know that is related to the underlined word.

1. . . . such as <u>self-reliance</u> and hard work   _____
2. . . . individual strength and <u>resourcefulness</u>   _____
3. . . . to <u>populate</u> the land   _____
4. . . . the westward <u>expansion</u>   _____
5. Mexican <u>cession</u> 1848   _____

B Compare answers with a classmate.

C Add any new words to your vocabulary notebook.

5 Thinking about the topic ⓡ

Discuss the following questions in a small group.

1. Why do Americans and people from other countries view the West romantically?
2. How are these romantic views related to the values you learned about in this chapter?

1 Predicting ℝ

Remember that reading the titles, subheadings, and the first sentence of each paragraph can help you predict what the text will be about.

A Read the titles, subheadings, and the first sentence of each paragraph of the text. Then look quickly at the photographs below and the art in the boxed text.

B With a partner, discuss what you think "The Business of Success" will be about.

2 Thinking about the topic ℝ

A Look more carefully at the photographs below. They show workplaces in the second half of the nineteenth century and the early twentieth century.

B With a small group of classmates describe:

- The kind of work these people were doing
- Their working conditions
- What you think their lives were like
- What kind of future you think these workers had

Reading 3

THE BUSINESS OF SUCCESS

Americans value hard work, and they also admire ambitious people who take risks to achieve material success. Throughout the nation's history, the biggest success stories have been people who started with very little but, with a good idea and hard work, became very rich and
5 successful. In the business world, we call such people *entrepreneurs*.

The rise of big business

In the middle of the nineteenth century, the United States seemed to be a land of endless opportunity for someone with a good idea who was eager to take risks and to work hard to make the idea successful. The country was rich in natural resources, such as coal, iron, oil, and
10 wood. The **Industrial Revolution**, which began in Europe in the late eighteenth century, had reached the United States, and there were small factories all across the country. It was a time of opportunity for entrepreneurs. Two entrepreneurs, Andrew Carnegie and John D. Rockefeller, who were extremely successful during this period, have
15 become symbols of American big business.

Industrial Revolution the introduction into the economy of machines to do work that had previously been done by hand

Andrew Carnegie came to the United States from Scotland when he was 12. His family was very poor. His first job was working in a factory for $1.20 a week. He saved his money carefully, invested it in various businesses, and made more money. While he was still in his
20 30s, Carnegie decided that the future of the country was in steel. He built a steel factory and his business was very successful, but Carnegie was not satisfied. He knew that if he reduced his competition, he would make even more money, and so he bought other steel companies. He also used a strategy called *vertical integration* to control all aspects of
25 steel production: He bought iron mines that supplied the steel mills, and he bought railroad companies that shipped the steel. In this way, he could control and profit from every part of the steel industry. Carnegie's company was the first to achieve this level of vertical integration. Soon, he became the richest man in the country.

30 The life of John D. Rockefeller offers a similar "rags-to-riches" (poor to rich) story. At the age of 16, Rockefeller started to work for a shipping company. He saved his money and invested it in the oil business. Like Carnegie, he understood the importance of vertical integration and of reducing competition. He controlled all aspects of
35 the oil industry: drilling, refining, and transportation. He wanted to decrease competition and increase his profit, and so he bought every small oil company that he could. By 1877, when Rockefeller was only 38 years old, his company, Standard Oil, controlled 90 percent of the oil industry in the country.

When one company controls all or almost all of an industry, such as steel or oil, it is called a *monopoly*. In the 1890s, the federal government took action to reduce the power of monopolies. However, the businesses of Carnegie, Rockefeller, and other major entrepreneurs remained large and successful in spite of the changes. The lives of these industry leaders illustrate many important American values. They worked hard; they were independent and self-reliant. However, they were also ruthless in their ambition and in their pursuit of material success. Some would say they illustrate the best and the worst of the American Dream.

Workers' rights: The rise of trade unions

Cartoon showing control of the industry and government by Standard Oil

These huge industries were partly responsible for helping to make the United States the most important economic power of the twentieth century. However, the success of big business in the nineteenth century was often at the expense of the workers. Many successful industrial entrepreneurs of the time believed that any business strategy was fair in the race for higher profits. This meant that frequently they did not treat their workers well.

One aspect of the Industrial Revolution was new technology that allowed machines to take the place of skilled craftsmen who had done much of the work by hand. The machines needed fewer and less-skilled workers to operate them, which meant that factories hired fewer people. Competition for the remaining jobs increased, and wages declined when new technology was introduced. The large number of immigrants coming into the United States and looking for factory work also increased the competition for jobs. The days were long and the pay was low, but industrial workers had very few alternatives. They had to take whatever work they could find.

Low wages and long hours were not the only problems that workers faced. Industrial workplaces were often dangerous: hot metal in the steel factories and dust in the mills caused injuries and disease. Workers had no protection, and they lost their jobs if they were injured or became sick and could not work. In the second half of the nineteenth century, the combination of these dangerous and difficult conditions and low wages encouraged the establishment of the labor movement, that is, the creation of **trade unions** to fight for and protect workers. Like many Americans before them, these workers also wanted an opportunity for material success – a chance to

trade union
organization of workers that protects their rights and represents them in such matters as pay and working conditions

achieve the American Dream. The unions promised them a chance to level the playing field. The struggle to create unions and expand their power was difficult and sometimes violent. Factory owners were often 85 opposed to the unions because they knew that strong unions would demand better pay and working conditions for their members, and better pay for workers would lower the company's profits.

In spite of the opposition of owners, unions continued to fight for the rights and protection of workers against powerful businesses. The 90 unions won many of these battles, and these victories helped to raise pay levels and expand benefits, such as health insurance and pensions, and make workplaces safer. Many of the favorable workplace conditions in the United States today are a result of the efforts of trade unions.

Women in the workforce

The workers in the big steel mills and big factories were all men, but women were also a major part of the labor force at the end of the nineteenth century and the beginning of the twentieth century. Women had fewer choices than men, and many of them ended up in sweatshops, or crowded rooms, where they sewed clothing for up to 16 hours a day. The working conditions were poor, but sweatshops gave many women an independent start in their new country. As in men's work, there was fierce competition for these jobs, which kept wages very low. The rooms where the women worked were cramped and hot. The piles of clothing and cloth made fire a constant danger. In 1911, a fire swept through a sweatshop in New York with 600 women inside. One hundred forty-five women and girls died in the fire. The tragedy led to new laws to protect workers.

Triangle Shirtwaist Company fire, 1911

1 Answering multiple-choice questions Ⓐ

Many tests are in multiple-choice format. Understanding the strategies for answering can help you on this kind of test. Study these guidelines.

- Read the question and think about the answer before you look at the choices. One of the choices might match the answer you thought of.
- Read the questions and the directions carefully. Each question may be a little bit different.
- Read all the choices carefully before you decide on your answer.
- Negative answers are more difficult to understand, so read them especially carefully.
- Cross out the choices that you know are wrong.
- A positive answer is more likely to be true than a negative answer.
- Answers with words like *never*, *always*, and *only* are often the wrong ones. Answers with words like *usually* and *often* are more likely to be correct.
- The longest answer is often the correct one.

Read each statement about the text and circle the correct answer. Use the strategies above to help you.

1. What characteristics do Andrew Carnegie and John D. Rockefeller share? Circle all of the correct answers.
    a. They began their lives poor, but they made a lot of money.
    b. They created monopolies.
    c. They didn't like taking risks.
    d. They controlled the oil industry.

2. A company owns cotton fields, cotton mills, and factories that make clothing from cotton. This is an example of
    a. entrepreneurship.
    b. a sweatshop.
    c. a monopoly.
    d. vertical integration.

3. According to the text, how did the introduction of technology affect workers?
    a. All of their workers lost their jobs.
    b. Factories did not need as many workers.
    c. Many workers joined unions.
    d. There was less competition among workers.

4. Why did workers join unions?
    a. Unions offered higher pay than factories.
    b. Unions helped workers find better jobs.
    c. Unions helped stop the violence in the factories.
    d. Unions fought for better pay and working conditions.

2 Writing about change ⓦ

Some verbs show direction of change, that is, whether something is going up or down or getting bigger or smaller. Some of these verbs show who or what controls the direction. Other verbs do not. Some can do both.

Controller must be stated	
raise (↑)	cut (↓)
	lower (↓)
	reduce (↓)

controller

Andrew Carnegie **reduced** his workers' pay in order to keep his steel mills profitable.
INCORRECT: Steel industry profits **reduced** at the end of the twentieth century.

Controller must not be stated	
go up (↑)	fall (↓)
rise (↑)	go down (↓)
grow (↑)	decline (↓)

[controller is not stated]

Union membership **rose** in the first half of the twentieth century.
INCORRECT: Unions **rose** workers' wages.

Controller may or may not be stated	
increase (↑)	decrease (↓)
expand (↑)	shrink (↓)

controller

Vertical integration **decreases** competition.
[controller is not stated]
Competition **decreases** if there are monopolies.

A Find these verbs of direction in the text. State what went up or down and, if possible, who or what controlled the upward or downward direction. If the controller is not stated, write an *X*.

Verb of direction	What went up or down?	Who/What controlled it?
reduced (Line 22)		
decrease (Line 36)		
reduce (Line 42)		
increased (Line 66)		
declined (Line 67)		
increased (Line 69)		
expand (Line 83)		
raise (Line 90)		
expand (Line 91)		

B Write three sentences of your own. Use any of the verbs in the box or in the chart in Step A. Describe trends you have read about in this chapter or in earlier chapters.

3 Collocations ⓥ

> Remember that some words often appear together. For example, some nouns frequently occur with specific verbs. In addition, these verbs often appear with a set of nouns with similar meanings. It is important to notice these word combinations.

A Find the nouns below in the text. Then find the verbs that are used with them. Write the verbs in the correct blanks. More than one verb may be used with some nouns.

1. _____ risks
2. _____ success
3. _____ , _____ , _____ money
4. _____ problems
5. _____ their jobs
6. _____ battles

B Verbs are often used with sets of nouns that have similar meaning. Match the verbs in Step A with the nouns below. Write the correct verb in the blank. Some verbs are used more than once.

1. _____ challenges
2. _____ a goal
3. _____ wars
4. _____ chances
5. _____ results
6. _____ hardships

C Choose two of the verb + noun collocations and write a new sentence for each.

4 Understanding cartoons ⓡ

> Remember that cartoons and other art can often express ideas more quickly than words.

A With a partner, look at the cartoon on page 172. Then answer the questions below.

1. Why did the artist choose an octopus to represent Standard Oil?
2. What are the buildings in the picture? What does the artist mean by this?
3. What is the artist's opinion of Standard Oil?

B With your partner, discuss this question: Can cartoons like this change public opinion?

Chapter 7 Academic Vocabulary Review

The following words appear in the readings in Chapter 7. They all come from the Academic Word List, a list of words that researchers have discovered occur frequently in many different types of academic texts. For a complete list of all the Academic Word List words in this chapter and in all the readings in this book, see the Appendix on page 206.

acquired	circumstances	images	invested
alternatives	consistent	implication	persisted
attitude	illustrate	injuries	preceded

Complete the sentences with words from the lists.

1. Poor equipment in mines and factories caused serious _____ and sometimes death.

2. The people who _____ money in the oil business made a substantial profit.

3. During the 1870s, Rockefeller _____ many small oil refineries.

4. The people who moved west of the Mississippi had a serious but optimistic _____ about their future.

5. Books and movies are filled with _____ of the American Dream. A house with a car in the driveway is just one example.

6. During the Civil War, the North had to find _____ to Southern cotton. They bought cotton from India and Russia instead.

7. The courts were not always _____ in their decisions about segregation. As a result, laws were sometimes in conflict.

8. One _____ of the cartoon is that the government had a role in the success of big oil, steel, and railroad companies.

9. Conflicts and violence often _____ the final agreements between the unions and the factory owners.

10. The dominance of Standard Oil _____ long after the government limited the power of its monopoly on the oil business.

Developing Writing Skills

In this chapter, you have read about the historical context of some fundamental American values. In this section, you will prepare to write a more formal writing assignment – an essay – by writing an introductory paragraph. You will use what you learn here in your final writing assignment at the end of the next chapter.

Introductory paragraphs

Academic essays have several parts. In previous writing assignments, you have been writing the middle part – the body paragraphs. In this assignment, you will work on the first part of an academic essay – the introduction. The introductory paragraph is very important because it tells the reader what the rest of the essay will be about and, even more important, tells the reader what you plan to say about the topic.

A With a partner or in a small group, discuss which of the themes in this chapter are the most important or have been most influential. Some themes are listed below. You may think of others, too. Take notes on your discussion.

- Egalitarianism
- Self-reliance
- Optimism
- Hard work
- Risk-taking
- Individualism
- Self-discipline

B Choose one theme to write about. We will call this "theme X."

C Why did you choose theme X? In what areas of American life and history has theme X had a strong influence? Review the topics that have been discussed in this chapter or in earlier chapters to find evidence of the influence of your theme. Possibilities include:

- Civil rights
- Business
- Westward expansion

Use the strategies you learned in Developing Writing Skills (pages 125–126). Collect evidence that will support the idea that theme X is important in these areas of American life and history.

D Review the information you collected. What are the two strongest pieces of evidence that support your claim? Highlight them in your notes. You will use them later.

E Now you are ready to write your introductory paragraph. Your topic is the importance of theme X in American life and history. An introductory paragraph should include the following elements:

- A general statement that introduces the topic
- A sentence that makes an important claim about the topic
- Several sentences that tell the reader what to expect in the rest of the essay

Study the paragraph below. It is about the theme of *innovation*, which is the use of new ideas and ways of doing things.

Americans have always looked ahead to what is modern and new. The spirit of invention and innovation has been an important theme throughout American history. Innovation has been particularly important in the development of American industry and advances in medicine. In both of these areas, the United States is a world leader because of constant innovation.

F With a partner, examine the paragraph above. Find the elements of a good introductory paragraph that are listed in Step E. Then answer these questions.

1. What is the author's claim?

_____

2. What do you expect that the next two paragraphs in this essay will be about?

_____

_____

G Write your own introductory paragraph. Use your notes on the two strongest pieces of evidence from Step D. Make sure you include all the required elements of an introductory paragraph.

H Exchange papers with a partner. Answer these questions about his or her paragraph.

1. What theme did your partner choose?

_____

2. What was your partner's claim?

_____

3. What two examples did your partner use to illustrate the influence of the theme?

   a. _____

   b. _____

4. Was your partner's claim convincing? Did the introductory paragraph indicate what the essay would be about? Why or why not?

_____

Chapter 8
American Values Today

Thinking about the topic ®

> Remember that reading the title and headings will help you think about the content of the text before you begin reading.

Work with a partner or in a small group to complete the following activities.

A Skim the reading and discuss these questions.

1. What "rights and responsibilities" do you think the title refers to?
2. Both headings contain *versus*. What does this term mean? If you do not know, look it up in a dictionary.
4. When could the rights of an individual conflict with the interests of a larger group of people? Describe the situation.
5. Many people feel that individuals should show self-reliance and not depend on assistance from others. Consider these questions and discuss examples.
   - Are there some situations in which this is not true?
     - Should individuals ever expect assistance from others in society?
     - Should individuals ever expect continual assistance from society?

B Complete the chart. List responsibilities of each group.

Responsibility of individuals	Responsibility of society	Responsibility of both individuals and society
Raising children		

C Explain your choices to your partner or group.

Reading 1

THE INDIVIDUAL AND SOCIETY: RIGHTS AND RESPONSIBILITIES

Individual rights are so important to Americans and so fundamental to the nation that they are part of the Bill of Rights. The Bill of Rights was written to defend the rights of individuals, to protect them from their
5 own government and against a rule of the majority. Yet a nation that allows all individuals to do whatever they want will soon fall apart. Individuals have rights but they also have responsibilities. It is also important to consider the good of the whole society.

10 A balance between the rights of individuals and the good of society, that is, the good of the whole nation, has been important throughout American history. Sometimes circumstances make it impossible for individuals to accept their responsibilities, and society must act to help those individuals who cannot help themselves. This is one of
15 the most important functions of government. Thus, the United States government has had to find a balance in two situations: (1) between protecting the rights of the individual and protecting the good of society, and (2) between encouraging self-reliance and providing support and assistance to people who need them.

Individual rights versus the good of society

20 Two situations in which the rights of the individual have conflicted with the good of society involve eminent domain and national security. The principle of eminent domain states that private individuals may be required to sell their property, including their homes, if the land is needed for a project that is for the good of society. For instance,
25 the government might want to build a railroad, a school, or a park on land where homes already stand. The owners of those homes receive a payment, but they must cede their property to the government.

The second situation concerns the balance between national security and individuals' freedom of speech and their expectation of privacy.
30 Most citizens do not expect the government to read their e-mail or listen to their telephone conversations. By law, if government officials want to do this, they must first get permission from a judge. Since September 11, 2001, however, the government has limited individual rights in these areas and expanded the power of the government to
35 gather information about private citizens. The government has argued that it must have this power in order to better protect national security.

Self-reliance versus government support and assistance

An important example of the need to balance self-reliance and government assistance is the federal government's response to the problems in a weak economy. For example, during the **Great** 40 **Depression** (1929–1940), almost a quarter of the population was unemployed. People lost their farms, their businesses, and even their homes. They could not rely on themselves; they needed help from the government. In 1933, President Franklin Roosevelt established the **New Deal**, which included many programs and new laws to provide 45 economic security for all members of society, especially the retired, the unemployed, and the poor. To provide jobs, the government paid unemployed workers to build roads, schools, and government buildings; it paid unemployed artists to paint, take photographs, write books, perform plays, and play music.

50 Seventy-five years later, during another economic crisis, many Americans were struggling economically. Many people had lost their jobs, and some had lost their homes. The government again responded with programs to help them and to help the economy recover. In 2009, as part of the American Recovery and Reinvestment Act (ARRA), the 55 government spent $275 billion to create new jobs and job-training programs, and another $224 billion to provide assistance and health care to people who had lost their jobs. The New Deal and the ARRA programs increased government assistance to individuals, but they also increased people's reliance on the government. Some Americans 60 believe that the government should do more to help people in need, but other Americans object to the high cost of government assistance programs, which rely on tax dollars.

Americans disagree on the role of the government in individuals' lives. Debates like these show the difficulty of balancing the needs of 65 individuals and those of society as a whole.

Great Depression a period in history (1929–1940) during which economic activity slowed dramatically, prices fell, and people lost jobs

New Deal a set of government programs that were established to help the United States recover from the Great Depression

Redistributing resources: Taxation

One of the functions of government is to provide services to the people who live in the country. This requires money. The money comes from different sources, but most of it comes from taxes. Taxation is a way of redistributing resources. In the United States, there are many different kinds of taxes, but there are three primary categories for individuals (businesses pay different kinds of taxes):

Taxes on what you earn: Generally, this is income tax based on earnings from work. Because this tax is a percentage of your income, as your income increases, the amount of tax you must pay also increases. Furthermore, the percentage generally increases as your income goes up. For example, in 2012, a person who earned $35,000 from a job paid tax at the rate of 15 percent, whereas a person who earned $200,000 per year paid at the rate of 33 percent. The federal government and many states have income taxes.

Taxes on what you own: This is property tax. If you own a house, an apartment, or a building, you must pay tax on it every year. In most communities, property tax is used to pay for schools. Property taxes are controlled by local communities like cities and towns.

Taxes on what you buy: This is called a sales tax. This kind of tax works somewhat differently from income and property taxes. An income tax is proportional, which means that rich people who have higher incomes should pay higher taxes. However, everyone pays the same sales tax on a pair of shoes or a computer. It does not matter if you are rich or poor. Sales taxes are controlled by the states.

Governments depend on these taxes. Without this money, they could not function.

1 Reading for main ideas ⓡ

A Read the statements. Check (✓) the sentence that states the main idea of the entire text.

_____ **1.** The main function of government is to protect individuals from society.

_____ **2.** The government must balance the needs of society and individuals.

_____ **3.** The important functions of government can be seen in the Bill of Rights.

B The text provides two key examples to support this main idea. What are they?

1. _____

2. _____

C The text provides two specific examples to support each key example of the main idea. List them below.

1. a. _____

   b. _____

2. a. _____

   b. _____

2 Applying what you have read ⓡ

A Review the information in the boxed text on taxation. Then read these statements about taxes.

_____ **1.** People who earn a lot of money should be able to keep it. The government should not take money away from people who work hard by making them pay taxes.

_____ **2.** Some people have problems that are not their own fault. For example, they may get very sick or the factory where they work may close down. They need and deserve help from the rest of us. Taxes can provide the money for that help.

_____ **3.** There are some things that individuals cannot do for themselves. We need the government to do things like fight against our enemies, provide police protection, and build roads and bridges. We need taxes to pay for that.

B Decide if each statement in Step A illustrates an argument for *a*, *b*, or *c* below. Write the letter in the correct blank.

a. The protection of individual rights

b. The good of the whole society

c. Assistance for those in need

3 Understanding text structure Ⓦ

Read the functions listed below. Match each function to a paragraph in the reading. Write the paragraph number(s) in the blank. Several paragraphs may match a single function.

_____ **1.** Establishes and explains the main idea

_____ **2.** Provides and explains an example

_____ **3.** Reviews previous information about the topic and provides background for the main idea

_____ **4.** Comments on the significance of the topic

4 Prepositions Ⓥ

Remember that some verbs frequently occur with specific prepositions. You should learn the verb + preposition(s) together.

A The following prepositions are used in the text with the verbs listed below. Match the prepositions with the verbs. More than one answer may be possible.

against	for	from	on	to	with

1. to protect people _____ / _____ something

2. to conflict _____

3. to listen _____

4. to rely _____

5. to object _____

6. to disagree _____

7. to pay _____

8. to depend _____

B Choose three of the verb + preposition combinations and write a sentence about rights or responsibilities with each.

5 Collocations Ⓥ

Remember that some verbs and nouns often appear together. In addition, these verbs can appear with a set of nouns with related meanings. It is important to notice these word combinations.

A Reread the text to find the nouns below. Then find the verbs that are used with them. Write the verbs in the correct blanks.

1. _____ responsibilities

2. _____ assistance

3. _____ permission

4. _____ information

5. _____ photographs

6. _____ plays

7. _____ music

8. _____ taxes

B The verbs in the box are also used with the nouns in **bold** from Step A. Complete each sentence with a verb from the box. One verb is used twice. Be sure to use the correct form of the verb.

> take   collect   need   give

1. The government _____ **information** about individuals that may be a threat to national security.
2. Most parents teach their children that it is important to _____ **responsibility** for their actions.
3. Both the state and federal government _____ **taxes** in order to pay for public services.
4. A judge must _____ **permission** before the police can search a person's car or house.
5. When the economy is weak or after a natural disaster, people often _____ **assistance** from the government.

C Check your answers with a classmate.

6 Responding to a quote Ⓐ

Some tests may ask you to respond to a quote. The quote will illustrate a basic point you have studied. In order to answer effectively, follow these steps.
- Study the quote carefully. Identify the speaker and the topic.
- Think about how the quote is related to the material you have been studying: Does it support or contradict a point?
- Try to use parts of the quote in your answer.
- Add your own ideas if the question asks for them.

A Work in a small group. Discuss the following quotation from Lyndon Johnson, the thirty-sixth president of the United States.

If government is to serve any purpose, it is to do for others what they are unable to do for themselves.   – February, 1964

B Review the main idea stated in Task 1 above. What part of the text is the quote related to? What examples in the reading illustrate the idea in the quote?

C Write a short-answer response. Show how this quote is related to ideas in the text.

D Exchange answers with a classmate.

1 Previewing art ⓡ

A Examine the photographs of the car below and the cars on pages 188–189.

B Discuss the following questions with a partner.

1. What do these images make you think of?
2. Where have you seen cars like these before?
3. Do you own a car? If so, is it similar to one in the photographs?
4. What do you use your car for? To go to work? To shop?
5. Do you think a car is mainly a convenience, a necessity, a symbol of your lifestyle, or something else?

2 Scanning ⓡ

A Scan the text to find the correct information.

1. How many cars were on American roads in 1930?	(Par. 2)	_____
2. What percentage of American families owned a car in 1960?	(Par. 3)	_____
3. What percentage of American families owned a car in 2010?	(Par. 3)	_____
4. How many miles of road were in the original Interstate Highway System?	(Par. 3)	_____
5. What kind of car became popular in the 1990s?	(Par. 4)	_____
6. How many miles did Americans drive in 2010?	(Par. 5)	_____

B Discuss the questions with a partner.

1. What will the text be about? How does the information from Step A connect to the topic of the text?
2. How important do you think cars are to people in the United States? Explain your answer.

Reading 2

THE OPEN ROAD AND CAR CULTURE

The road and the automobile have long been symbols of Americans' love of the freedom of wide-open spaces. Americans feel that driving a car means the freedom to come and go wherever they choose, whenever they choose. Rising gasoline prices, traffic jams, and air pollution have
5 not kept Americans off the road.

At the beginning of the twentieth century, cars were for rich people, and roads were rough and not well maintained. Over the next decades, several factors made it possible for millions of Americans to participate in "car culture." First, the price of cars dropped significantly
10 because of new technology and new methods for manufacturing cars. The discovery of oil in the state of Texas brought down the price of gasoline as well. Still, in 1930, there were fewer than 5 million cars on American roads.

After World War II, the economy of the United States began to
15 grow. The soldiers came home, and they wanted to start families. Many of them bought homes outside of the cities, in the suburbs, where lots of houses were available at a reasonable price. Most people needed to drive because there was little public transportation from the suburbs to their jobs in the city. This situation created the need for more roads.
20 In 1956, Congress established the Interstate Highway System, with more than 42,000 miles of roads. More roads meant more people

could reach their jobs in the cities from the suburbs, so more people decided to move to the suburbs. Owning a car became essential for daily life. The number of cars
25 on the road went up by 50 percent from 40 million to 60 million. By 1960, 77 percent of all American families had at least one car. In 2010, the figure was over 90 percent. In fact, the average American household has more cars and trucks than drivers!

30 Cars are not just for transportation, however. The kind of car you have can say a lot about who you are – or who you want to be. During the 1950s, American cars became bigger and more stylish. Young people in small towns and suburbs spent their evenings in cars, driving
35 up and down the streets. Books and movies made cars and life on the road seem glamorous. Forty years later, SUVs (sport-utility vehicles) became very popular, often with young people. They reminded buyers of a traditional American image: a self-reliant individual
40 with a free and active life. SUVs made owners feel as if they were ready for life in the wilderness. SUVs

became popular for these reasons even though many SUV owners simply drove their cars to work every day. More recently, the popularity of SUVs has declined, partly because they use a lot of gasoline. Many
45 people want to show they are concerned about the environment and saving energy. As a result, electric cars, and hybrid cars, which use both gasoline and electricity, have risen in popularity. In one survey, hybrid car owners were asked why they had bought their cars. Their reply on this survey: "It makes a statement about me." As in the past,
50 these cars are often not just for transportation; they often symbolize who you are.

Cars styles go in and out of fashion, but with 250 million cars across the country, Americans are still in love with their cars and the open road. In 2010, they drove more than 3 trillion miles.

Afoot and light-hearted, I take to the open road,
Healthy, free, the world before me,
The long brown path before me, leading wherever I choose.

– "Song of the Open Road," Walt Whitman (1890)

Irv Gordon, 70, drove almost 3 million miles around the country in his 1966 Volvo.

1 Answering true/false questions Ⓐ

Remember to use the strategies for answering true/false questions on page 81.

A Read the statements about the text. Write *T* (true) or *F* (false) for each statement.

_____ **1.** Higher gas prices and heavy traffic have reduced driving in the   _____
        United States.

_____ **2.** New technology helped reduce the price of cars in the early
        twentieth century.   _____

_____ **3.** The growth of the suburbs led to an increase in car ownership.   _____

_____ **4.** The construction of the U.S. Interstate Highway System encouraged
        people to buy cars.   _____

_____ **5.** Only 10 percent of the people in the United States do not own a car.   _____

_____ **6.** SUVs use gas very efficiently.   _____

_____ **7.** Hybrid cars use gas very efficiently.   _____

_____ **8.** There were 10 times as many cars on U.S. roads in 2010 than in 1930.   _____

B After each statement in Step A, write the number of the paragraph(s) where you found the information.

2 Reading for details Ⓡ

A According to the text, car ownership rose considerably between World War II and 1960. The four events below led to this increase. In what order did they occur? Order the events 1–4. Write the correct number in the blank.

_____ The government built good roads so people could get from their homes to their jobs in the city.

_____ More people moved to the suburbs because there were lots of good roads.

_____ People moved to the suburbs where there were good, inexpensive houses.

_____ People who lived in the suburbs needed cars because there was little public transportation.

B Compare your answers with a partner.

3 Writing about reasons Ⓦ

Because and *because of* both indicate that a reason will follow, but they have different functions in a sentence.

- *Because* links two clauses.

    clause   clause

    Many factories closed **because** costs were too high.

- *Because of* is a preposition, so it links a clause with a noun/noun phrase.

    clause   noun/noun phrase

    Many factories closed **because of** the high costs.

A Go back to the text. Find one sentence with *because of*. Circle *because of* and underline the noun phrase it links to. Now find two sentences with *because*. Circle *because* and underline the clause that contains the reason.

B Complete the sentences with *because* or *because of*. If the sentence already has *because* or *because of*, use your own words to complete the sentence. If you need more space, write your answers on a separate piece of paper.

  1. Some Europeans immigrated to the United States *because of* _____ .

  2. Some businesses hire undocumented workers _____ they can pay them lower wages.

  3. Many African Americans could not vote _____ literacy tests and voting taxes.

  4. After the legal case of *Brown versus Board of Education of Topeka*, some communities closed their public schools *because* _____ .

  5. Some people buy big cars *because of* _____ .

  6. Andrew Carnegie opposed the trade unions _____ he knew they wanted higher pay for workers.

4 Gerunds Ⓦ

> A *gerund* is the *-ing* form of a verb that is used as noun. A gerund is used when the grammar requires a noun, but the meaning requires something more active like a verb. Gerunds can be used as the subject or object of a sentence or as an object of a preposition. The gerund allows you to use the meaning of verbs in these two noun positions.
>
> ***Carrying*** *a gun is legal in many states.* (subject)
> *Some people object to **paying** taxes for government programs.* (object of preposition)

A Find these gerunds in the text and highlight them. Were the gerunds used as a subject (S) or after a preposition (P)? Write *S* or *P* in the blank.

1. driving (Line 2) _____   **3.** owning (Line 23) _____

2. manufacturing (Line 10) _____   **4.** saving (Line 46) _____

B Complete the sentences with the gerund form of an appropriate verb.

1. For many teenagers, _____ to drive is an important step toward becoming an adult.

2. _____ two cars is very common in the United States.

3. The federal government is responsible for _____ major highways.

4. _____ people who cannot help themselves is one of the main functions of government.

5. SUVs are built for _____ in the mountains and on dirt roads.

5 Applying what you have read Ⓡ

A Discuss the following questions with a partner or in a small group.

1. Explain the meaning of this excerpt from the text:
". . . cars are often not just for transportation; they can say a lot about who you are – or who you want to be."

2. In what ways to do you think car culture is connected to Americans' "love of the open road"?

3. How is the "love of the open road" connected to other themes you have read about in this unit?

B Read the verse at the end of the text. It is the beginning of a longer poem, "Song of the Open Road," by Walt Whitman, one of the nation's greatest poets. With your group, discuss how Whitman's ideas are connected to the theme of the text.

1 Conducting a survey Ⓐ

Surveys are used to gather information about people's opinions and behaviors. They are frequently used in academic research. You may need to conduct a survey to collect information for an assignment.

A The text you are going to read, "Is the American Dream Still Possible?" is about factors that are important for success in life. With a partner, discuss what factors you think are important for succeeding or "getting ahead."

B Survey your classmates' views about the factors.

On a separate piece of paper, make a chart like the one below. Ask each classmate to rate the importance of the factors for success. Check (✓) your classmate's response in the appropriate column for each factor.

Factors in getting ahead	Essential	Very important	Somewhat important	Not very important	Not important at all
Wealthy family					
Knowing important people					
Natural ability and talent					
Good education					
Hard work					

C Count your results. Calculate a percentage of answers for each factor.

2 Examining graphics Ⓡ

A Study Figure 8.1 on page 195. The term *economic mobility* is another way of saying *getting ahead*.

B With a partner, compare the percentages in Figure 8.1 with the results of your survey. The categories in the two surveys are not exactly the same, but there are many similarities. Then answer the questions below.

1. Did the people in your survey think they can control whether they get ahead?

2. In what ways are your survey results and the results of the Pew study similar? How are they different?

Reading 3

IS THE AMERICAN DREAM STILL POSSIBLE?

Owning your own home has always been a symbol of the American Dream.

Is it still possible to achieve the American Dream? The answer depends on how you define "American Dream." Americans generally explain its meaning in one ⁵ of two ways. Some say it means having freedom and living in a society based on equality; however, most think it means achieving economic security and success. In other words, the American Dream ¹⁰ means having upward economic and social mobility, that is, improving your financial and social situation. Americans have always believed that success is a result of a person's individual ability and ¹⁵ hard work as well as access to education and opportunity. They see the United States as a meritocracy, that is, a system in which individuals are rewarded for their ability and effort, not for their family background, wealth, or connections to powerful people. ²⁰ Generally, Americans believe people can control their own success.

In the history of the United States, almost every generation has been able to achieve upward mobility; each generation has been more successful than the previous one. Starting at the end of the twentieth century, however, upward mobility became more difficult because of ²⁵ changes in the economy and the rising cost of college tuition. There is also considerable evidence that the income gap between rich and poor has increased in the last 30 years. In other words, the poor are getting poorer, and the rich are getting richer.

Until recently, the United States was a major producer of goods, ³⁰ with many natural resources, plentiful labor, and advanced technology. All of these made the country an efficient and powerful economic and political force in the world. Today, however, the economic role of the United States has changed. It is no longer a major producer nation; instead, it is a major consumer nation. Many of the jobs that gave ³⁵ people the opportunity for upward mobility were in manufacturing, but these jobs are gone now.

There has been another important change – in the perception of the role of education. Many Americans have thought of education as a democratic process, allowing children of all backgrounds equal access to opportunity. They have seen education alone as a path to economic success. Today, more than ever, education is necessary to get a job that pays well. However, many Americans recognize now that education alone may not be a certain path to success for their children. Not every child gets an equal education or the chance to succeed that education can often bring.

The American educational system does not always provide as much support for poor children as for children from high-income families. Public schools are paid for mostly with property tax dollars from states and cities. The taxes are based on property values, which means that people pay taxes based on the value of their homes. Sadly, as poor communities become poorer, the value of their homes decreases, and these communities cannot collect enough tax money to pay for good schools. In addition, a college education, which was once within reach for many Americans, has become too expensive for many students. Thus, an important path to economic success – a good education – may be lost.

Americans have begun to ask if it is still possible for each new generation to move up the economic ladder, that is, to have a better life than their parents. For the first time, there is considerable downward mobility in the population. Many say they work harder than their parents did, but they do not feel financially secure. Americans save very little – less than 5 percent of their income. This is far less than in most other countries. As a result, if something bad happens – if a parent loses his or her job or if a family member gets sick – most families have very little protection.

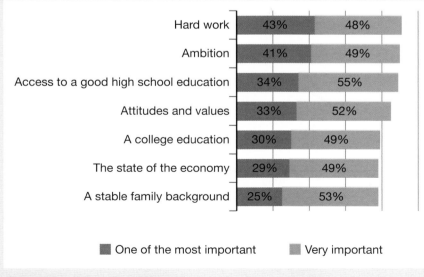

Figure 8.1 Factors in Economic Mobility

Source: **Pew study on economic mobility**

In spite of this trend, many Americans continue to show their traditional optimism. Many still believe that things will get better for them and for their children. More than two-thirds of the people in a major 2011 survey said they had either achieved the American Dream

70 or they believed that they would achieve it in their lifetime. When they were asked if they thought their children's standard of living would be as good or better than theirs, again, two-thirds of them said yes. The survey results suggest that most Americans still believe that individuals control their own success and that the most important

75 factors in getting ahead are hard work, personal ambition, and access to a good education (see Figure 8.1).

Education and upward mobility

Education has been an important path to the American Dream. Today, this means a college education. In the recent past, this meant a high school education. Fifty years ago, there were jobs in factories for workers without a college education; however, many of those factories have now closed because manufacturing is cheaper in countries where workers earn less money. Most jobs with higher pay in the twenty-first century require at least some higher education. Therefore, more Americans are going to college than ever before. In 2009, more than 20 million high school graduates enrolled in college, almost 10 times more than in 1950.

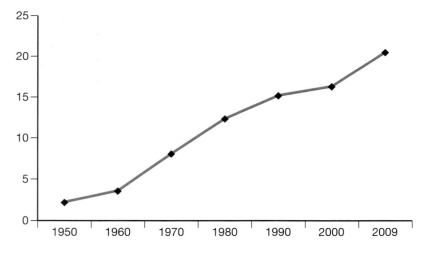

Enrollment in Higher Education (in millions)

1 Reading actively ®

Remember that to understand and remember what you have read, you need to read actively. Reading actively means responding to cues in the text. Cues such as *first*, *second*, *however*, and *some* indicate the relationship among parts and help you to predict what will come next. Other cues such as repeated words, synonyms, *this*, and *these* link ideas that occur frequently through the text. Active readers respond to cues and ask questions to find out what the cues are pointing to. Use these strategies to be an active reader.

- Notice each cue in the text.
- Ask yourself questions that the cue raises.
- Find the answers to the questions in the text.

A Study the chart. Find the cues in the text. Use the strategies in the box and the chart to ask questions. Go to the Actions column to find answers in the text. Highlight the answers.

Cues	Questions for active readers	Actions
The answer depends on how you define "**American Dream.**" (Line 2)	How many ways is it defined? Is there a key definition?	Find out how people define the **American Dream**. Find out the key definition (how most people define it).
Most think it means **achieving economic security and success.** (Line 7)	What do these terms mean? Why are they important?	Go forward to find the meaning. Consider the context to find the importance.
However, . . . (Line 24)	What is the contrast to this history?	Scan ahead to find it.
. . . **changes in the economy** and **inequalities in the educational systems** (Line 25)	What about the economy? What about education? These will be major themes I need to look for.	Start with the first theme. Find out what has **changed** in the **economy**.
All of **these** . . . (Line 31)	What are *these*?	Go back and find them.
another important change . . . (Line 37)	Are we moving to the second theme?	Scan ahead to find out. Look for something about **education**.
Not every child . . . (Line 43)	What is the contrast? What about other children?	Look for references to other **children**.
Thus, an important path . . . (Line 55)	Is this a conclusion? Is this the end of the second theme?	Scan ahead to find out.
Americans have begun **to ask** . . . (Line 57)	Why are they asking this?	Look for reasons.
this trend (Line 66)	What trend?	Look back to find it.

B Now read the chart below and use the same strategies as in Step A. Find the cues in the boxed text. Decide what the action should be. Write it in the third column. Highlight in the boxed text the information that you find.

Cues	Questions for active readers	Action
Education and **upward mobility** (Title)	This is the title, so it must be the topic. What is the relationship between them?	
In the recent **past** . . . (Line 2)	Does this mean I will also learn about the present?	
however, . . . (Line 3)	What is the contrast to this history?	
Most jobs with higher pay in the twenty-first century **require at least some higher education.** (Line 5)	Why is this important? What are the implications of this statement?	

2 Word families Ⓥ Ⓦ

Remember that in academic texts, writers often use related nouns and adjectives. Adding the suffix *-y* or *-(i)ty* changes an adjective to a noun.

Read the adjective and noun forms of words from the text in the chart below. Then choose the correct form to complete the sentences that follow.

Adjective	Noun
able	ability
certain	certainty
equal	equality
mobile	mobility
poor	poverty
secure	security

1. Many Americans invest part of their income for their future. They want to be financially _____ after they stop working.
2. _____ is the biggest barrier to educational achievement. Poor children are often less successful in school than children from middle-class families.
3. The American population has always been very _____ . Workers often move to a new city to find a better job.
4. It is impossible to predict with _____ what the economic future of the country will be.
5. One measure of a government's success is its _____ to help its poorest citizens.
6. Schools in rich and poor neighborhoods are rarely _____ .

3 Writing definitions Ⓦ

There is more than one way to define a term. Many terms are defined in the simple XYZ formula. Another formula uses gerunds. Gerunds are often used in definitions of concepts that include some kind of action. Remember that gerunds (the *-ing* form of the verb) are used when the meaning requires an action but the grammar requires a noun. Definitions with gerunds often use the verb *mean*.

term   definition using gerund
Self-reliance *means* depending on yourself, not other people.

term   definition using gerund
Poverty *means* not making enough money for basic necessities, such as food and shelter.

A Review the instructions for writing definitions using the XYZ formula (X is a Y that Z) on page 22.

B Write a one-sentence definition of each of these key terms from the text. Use the XYZ formula and your own words.

1. A *meritocracy* is a system that _____ .

2. A *property tax* is a tax that _____ .

3. A *consumer nation* is a country that _____ .

C Write definitions using gerunds.

1. Review the text and underline the three definitions of "American Dream" that use *mean(s)* + a gerund.

2. Write a one-sentence definition for each of the terms below using *mean(s)* + a gerund.

   a. upward mobility

   _____

   _____

   b. optimism

   _____

   _____

   c. self-discipline

   _____

   _____

   d. vertical integration

   _____

   _____

Chapter 8 Academic Vocabulary Review

The following words appear in the readings in Chapter 8. They all come from the Academic Word List, a list of words that researchers have discovered occur frequently in many different types of academic texts. For a complete list of all the Academic Word List words in this chapter and in all the readings in this book, see the Appendix on page 206.

available	generation	proportional	survey
consumers	previous	recovered	trend
financial	project	style	vehicles

Complete the sentences with words from the lists.

1. The number of people elected to the House of Representative is _____ to the population of each state.

2. The unemployment rate decreased after the economy _____ .

3. The number of _____ on the road increases every year.

4. In 1980, the price of gasoline was 50 percent higher than the price in the _____ decade.

5. Businesses hope that _____ will read their advertisements and buy their products.

6. When you invest money, it is important to read the _____ news regularly.

7. The size and _____ of cars have changed a great deal since World War II.

8. When the economy is weak, very few new jobs are _____ , especially for unskilled workers.

9. The newspaper conducted a _____ of its readers to find out their political views.

10. The most recent _____ is hybrid cars that use both gas and electricity. Cars that use a lot of gas are no longer very popular.

Practicing Academic Writing

In this unit, you have read about values that are the basis of many aspects of American life. You have learned that some of these values are the foundation of basic American hopes and goals. In this assignment, you will write a short essay on the following topic:

The foundation of the American dream

Which values are at the foundation of the American Dream? You will choose two values or beliefs that you believe are the most basic and important. You will develop these ideas in a four-paragraph essay that includes an introductory paragraph and a conclusion.

PREPARING TO WRITE

Gathering information

Before you begin a writing assignment, it is important to gather information to accomplish the task. Remember that there are different ways to gather information.

- Discuss the material or background for the assignment with classmates.
- Reread the material you are being asked to write about.
- Take notes on what you hear and what you read.

A Discuss the assignment in a small group. Take notes on your discussion. Consider the following questions.

1. How do Americans define and describe the American Dream?
2. Why is the American Dream important?
3. What are the basic values and beliefs that are at the heart of the American Dream?

B Based on your discussion and your understanding of the readings, follow these steps.

- Choose two values or beliefs to write about.
- Decide which of the two is more important.

C Now look back at the readings in this unit. Gather more information. Find specific support for your claim about the importance of these two values. Take notes and organize your information. You will use these notes to write the body paragraphs (Para. 2 and 3) of your essay.

D Make a brief outline for your body paragraphs. One has been started for you.

II. Value 1 _____

    A. Name and explain one value you have chosen.

    B. Explain why it is fundamental to the American Dream. This is your claim.

    C. Give at least one specific example from your reading or one that you are familiar with from outside of the texts.

III. Value 2 _____

    A. Name and explain the other value you have chosen.

    B. Explain why it is fundamental to the American Dream. This is your claim.

    C. Give at least one specific example from your reading or one that you are familiar with from outside of the texts.

E Now consider your introductory paragraph. Remember: An opening paragraph should include the following elements:

- A general statement that introduces the topic
- A sentence that makes an important claim about the topic
- Several sentences that tell the reader what to expect in the rest of the essay
- How will you write the introduction to your essay? Look back at your discussion notes from Step A and the questions you discussed. The answers to those questions should help you plan the three elements of your opening paragraph.

NOW WRITE

What do you write first?

> Is it best to begin at the beginning? Sometimes it is, but it can be easier to begin in the middle. When you begin with your introduction, you must say what will come next. However, you may not be sure of exactly what you want to say in the body. Writing the body first can tell you what to say in your introduction.

A Complete the following steps to write the body paragraphs for your essay.

    1. Review your outline from Step D. Think about how to order your information. Do you want to start or end with the more important value that you chose in Preparing to Write?

    2. Now write. Use your outline to write one paragraph for each value.

    3. Be sure each paragraph includes these elements:

- An introduction (Remember: your reader may not know about this value.)
- A topic sentence (a claim about the value's significance to the American Dream)
- Support for your claim in the form of reasons and examples

B Now that you are sure of the body content, you can write the introduction to your essay. Your introductory paragraph should answer the questions below. Some ideas for how to begin each element are included in parentheses.

- What is the American Dream? (*The American Dream means . . .*)
- What has been the significance of the American Dream in American history and culture? (*This dream has been important because . . .*)
- What are some general ideas about the beliefs and values that are basic to the American Dream? (*The American Dream is a complex idea that includes . . .*)
- Your claim about the two **most important themes** in the American Dream
  (*Throughout the history of the nation, the two most important . . .*)

C Put your introductory and body paragraphs together and read them over. You may notice that your essay ends somewhat suddenly. Most academic essays include a final paragraph that concludes the writer's argument.

Conclusions

For short pieces of writing, conclusions are usually also quite short, but they should remind the reader of your claim and also signal – not directly state – that this is the end of your text.

D Work with a partner. Reread the following concluding paragraphs of the first two texts in this chapter. What do you notice about them?

(8.1) Americans disagree on the role of the government in individuals' lives. Debates like these show the difficulty of balancing the needs of individuals and society as a whole.

(8.2) Car styles go in and out of fashion, but with 250 million cars across the country, Americans are still in love with their cars and the open road. In 2010, they drove more than 3 trillion miles.

There are three important things to notice about these conclusions.

- They are very short. You do not need to write a whole paragraph, especially for very short pieces of writing.
- They remind the reader of the main claim on the reading.
- They do not directly state that they are conclusions.
- They do not simply repeat the topic sentence or summarize the reading. Instead, they make a comment or add an interesting point.

E Now write a short concluding paragraph for your essay.

AFTER YOU WRITE

A Reread your own essay and check that:

- the introductory paragraph explains the American Dream and makes a claim about it;
- the body paragraphs contain clear topic sentences and support; and
- the conclusion doesn't simply repeat the topic sentence.

B Next, check for order of ideas and structure.

1. Think about how you introduced your essay and key point topics. Did you use chronological **cues** such as *The first belief is . . . , The second value is . . .* ? You can also choose more interesting signals. Consider this example from Reading 3 "The Business of Success" in Chapter 7:

Last sentence of introduction: ***Two entrepreneurs, Andrew Carnegie and John D. Rockefeller***, *who were extremely successful during this period, have become symbols of American big business.*

First sentence of body paragraph: ***Andrew Carnegie*** *came to the United States from Scotland when he was 12. His family was very poor.*

First sentence of next body paragraph: *The life of* **John D. Rockefeller** *offers a* ***similar*** *"rags-to-riches" (poor to rich) story.*

Notice the repetition of names and comparison cue. These introduce the topics and show that they are important. The writer names two entrepreneurs (Carnegie and Rockefeller) and then repeats each name to begin discussing that person's accomplishments. The comparison cue *similar* connects the discussion of the second example to that of the first.

2. Now think about how you connected other ideas. Did you include transitions to indicate which key point or example is more important and to link ideas within each paragraph?

C Exchange papers with a partner. Discuss the following questions about your essays:

- Does your partner's first sentence provide some background or explanation of what the essay will be about?
- Does the introductory paragraph make a claim for the values to be discussed?
- Has your partner written good topic sentences for each body paragraph?
- Does your partner appropriately support the claim about each value?
- Does your partner's essay include a brief but effective conclusion?

E Revise your work. Use you partner's suggestions and your own ideas.

F Edit your essay.

Reread your essay for spelling mistakes, punctuation errors, subject-verb agreement errors, incorrect use of past tense, and article usage. Make corrections if you find errors.

Appendix

Academic Word List vocabulary

accommodate
achieve
acquire
alternative
approximately
assistance
attitude
authorities
available
benefits
challenge
circumstance
consistent
consist
construction
consumer
contribute
controversial
cooperation
cycle
debate (v)
decline (v)
distribute
document
dominant
establishment
estimate (v)
eventually
evident
exclude
facility
financial

founder
framework
fundamental
furthermore
generation
guarantee
identity
illustrate
images
immigrant
implication
impose
incident
income
individual
inherently
injury
integrate
invest
issues
maintain
majority
media
minimum
occupation
participate
persist
perspectives
physical
policy
precede
predict

previous
primarily
principle
project
promotion
proportional
purchases (n)
pursuit
range
recover
reject
remove
resident
resource
restriction
revolutionary
section
security
specify
stable
status
style
survey
survive
target
transportation
trend
vehicle
violation
visibility
volunteer
widespread

Skills Index

Credits

The authors and publishers acknowledge the following sources of copyright material and are grateful for the permissions granted. While every effort has been made, it has not always been possible to identify the sources of all the material used, or to trace all copyright holders. If any omissions are brought to our notice, we will be happy to include the appropriate acknowledgements on reprinting.

Text Credits

Page 44: Text adapted from 'Hampton man allegedly killed in self-defense ID'd' by Erika Reif, *The Virginian-Pilot* © 2002. Used by permission.

Page 63: Excerpt of an interview with Fountain Hughes from *The Emergence of Black English*, edited by Guy Bailey et al, 1991. With kind permission by John Benjamins Publishing Company, Amsterdam/Philadelphia, www.benjamins.com.

Page 117: Excerpts reprinted by arrangement with The Heirs to the Estate of Martin Luther King Jr., c/o Writers House as agent for the proprietor New York, NY. "I Have a Dream." Copyright © 1963 by Dr. Martin Luther King, Jr. Renewed © 1991 by Coretta Scott King. "I've Been to the Mountaintop." Copyright © 1968 by Dr. Martin Luther King, Jr. Renewed © 1996 by Coretta Scott King.

Page 120: Text "Dream Deferred --- actual title is Harlem [2]" from *The Collected Poems of Langston Hughes* by Langston Hughes, edited by Arnold Rampersad with David Roessel, Associate Editor, copyright © 1994 by the Estate of Langston Hughes. Used by permission of Alfred A. Knopf, an imprint of the Knopf Doubleday Publishing Group, a division of Penguin Random House LLC. All rights reserved; Reprinted by permission of Harold Ober Associates. Copyright 1994 by the Langston Hughes Estate.

Illustration Credits

Page 28: Mark Duffin

Page 34, 35, 54, 61, 70, 80, 84, 85, 86, 89, 92, 144, 166, 195, 196: Kamae Design

Page 93, 97: Creators, www.creators.com. By permission of Steve Kelley and Creators Syndicate, Inc.

Photography Credits

1 ©Zack Frank/Shutterstock; 4 ©Bettmann/Corbis; 6 (*top to bottom*) ©GL Archive/Alamy; ©Robert Pernell/Shutterstock; 9 (*left to right*) ©Edwin Verin/Shutterstock; ©Nikreates / Alamy; 11 (*top to bottom*) ©AFP/Getty Images; ©Orhan Cam/Shutterstock; 12 ©Chip Somodevilla/Getty Images; 18 ©North Wind Picture Archives/Alamy; 19 ©Interfoto/Alamy; 23 ©Peeradach Rattanakoses/Shutterstock; 27 (*left to right*) ©AFP/Getty Images; ©William Campbell/Sygma/Corbis; 29 ©Spencer Platt/Getty Images; 30 ©Photo by Adam Bouska, Courtesy of NOH8 Campaign (www.NOH8Campaign. com); 36 (*top to bottom*) ©moodboard/Corbis; ©Laura Weisman Apaimages/APA Images/Zuma Wire Service/ Alamy; ©Ponizak/Caro/Alamy; ©Hemis.fr/Superstock; 40 (*clockwise from left to right*) ©Paul Bradbury/OJO Images Ltd/Alamy; ©Jochen Tack/Alamy; ©Michael Kemp/Alamy; 41 ©Kai-Uwe Och/Colouria Media/Alamy; 51 ©Özgür Donmaz/iStockphoto; 55 ©Bettmann/Corbis; 56 ©The Granger Collection, NYC - All rights reserved.; 57 (*left and right*) ©The Granger Collection, NYC - All rights reserved.; 60 (*clockwise from left to right*) ©Bettmann/Corbis; ©Universal Images Group/Getty Images; ©Historical/Corbis; 62 ©Library of Congress; 63 ©Library of Congress; 68 (*left to right*) ©Archive Photos/Getty Images; ©David McNew/ Getty Images; 71 ©aques Langevin/AP Images; 78 ©David McNew/Getty Images; 83 (*left to right*) ©lazlo/Shutterstock; ©Ekaterina Pokrovsky/Shutterstock; ©tratong/Shutterstock; 87 ©Splash News/Corbis; 90 ©AFP/Getty Images/Getty Images; 91 ©Sandy Huffaker/Getty Images; 94 ©Les Stone/ Sygma/Corbis; 103 ©Time & Life Pictures//Getty Images; 105 ©Bettmann/Corbis; 107 ©Todd Taulman/Shutterstock; 108 ©North Wind Picture Archives/Alamy; 111 (*left to right*) ©Bob Adelman/Historical Premium/Corbis; ©Hulton Archive/ Getty Images; 113 ©A'Lelia Bundles/Madam Walker Family Archives/madamcjwalker.com; 116 ©Bill Hudson/AP Images; 117 ©Flip Schulke/Historical Premium/Corbis; 118 ©AP Images; 119 ©Bettmann/Corbis; 120 ©Robert W. Kelley/ Time & Life Pictures/Getty Images; 123 ©Keystone-France/ Gamma-Keystone via Getty Images; 127 ©Stephen Chernin/ Getty Images; 128 ©Rob Lewine/Getty Images; 130 ©Roger Ressmeyer/Historical/Corbis; 134 (*clockwise from left to right*) ©Big Cheese Photo/Alloy/Corbis; ©Najlah Feanny/ Corbis News/Corbis; ©Michael Preston/Demotix/Corbis Wire/Corbis; 136 ©Image Source/Superstock; 137 ©aquatic creature/Shutterstock; 142 (*left to right*) ©Nicholas Kamm/ AFP/Getty Images; ©MCT via Getty Images; ©Thomas Samson/Gamma-Rapho via Getty Images; 145 ©Lisa Maree Williams/Getty Images; 153 ©kavram/Shutterstock; 155 (*left to right*) ©Kirn Vintage Stock/Retro/Corbis; ©Bettmann/ Corbis; ©Ivy Close Images/Alamy; 158 ©J. Howard Miller/ Fine Art/Corbis; 163 (*left to right*) ©Niday Picture Library/ Alamy; ©Danita Delimont/Getty Images; 164 ©Bettmann/ Corbis; 165 © North Wind Picture Archives/Alamy; 169 © North Wind Picture Archives/Alamy; 170 (*left to right*) ©Bettmann/Corbis; ©Baldwin H. Ward & Kathryn C. Ward/ Corbis; 172 ©Library of Congress; 173 ©Keystone/Hulton Archive/Getty Images; 181 ©Justin Sullivan/Getty Images; 182 ©Bettmann/Corbis; 187 ©Mark Elias/Bloomberg via Getty Images; 188 (*top to bottom*) ©Tom Wood/Alamy; ©Artostock.com/Alamy; 189 ©Getty Images; 194 ©Denise Kappa/Shutterstock